PRAISE FOR *THE CAREGIVER'S COMPASS*

"Holly's sensitive intuitiveness and careful questioning are the hallmark of her exceptional ability to coach, and they are the hallmarks of *The Caregiver's Compass*. Applying life coaching principles to this arena of caregiving is brilliant. This book is such a gift for us all, to have at our fingertips these coaching techniques to use at such a sensitive time."
—Sydney Rice-Harrild M.Ed., President, The Boston Coaching Company

"*The Caregiver's Compass* is a practical guide for those experiencing the role reversals of caring for an elderly parent. It provides positive ways to deal with the many changes that are taking place, sometimes with amazing speed! A focus on the opportunities and challenges of caregiving encourages the reader to change former ways of thinking and doing, and instead to stick to goals and embrace possibilities. Holly entered my life at such an important time. Her input has been invaluable."
—Cindy Baker, Caregiver for her mother with Alzheimers

"Ms. Whiteside's book is truly a compass for others. Her vision is leading edge, her span touching much more than this topic might suggest. She illuminates the landscape for us so well that we begin to see absolutely new directions that are possible for the human spirit through presence of mind, and compassionate, conscious connection."
—Pamela Greene MSW, Retired Imago Psychotherapist

D1441653

Be like the bird that,
passing on her flight awhile
on boughs too slight,
feels them give way beneath her,
and yet sings, knowing that she hath wings.

—Victor Hugo

THE CAREGIVER'S COMPASS

HOW TO NAVIGATE WITH
BALANCE & EFFECTIVENESS
USING MINDFUL CAREGIVING

HOLLY WHITTELSEY WHITESIDE

Cover Design ©2010 Holly Whittelsey Whiteside
Hummingbird photo original, by Robin Rodvold

Dedication quote is from "i carry your heart with me (i carry it in," by E. E. Cummings

ISBN: 1-44959-936-2

Author: Holly Whittelsey Whiteside
Email: MindfulCaregiving@comcast.net
Blog: http://transformingcaregiving.blogspot.com

The Totemic Meaning of the Hummingbird*

Hummingbird brings endurance for long journeys, teaching us simple courage. She symbolizes freedom, energy, tireless joy, and accomplishing things that are said to be impossible. In Incan theology, Hummingbird is the archetype for when thoughts and life/action become epic.

Hummingbird teaches us to hover in the moment, to appreciate its sweetness. We learn from her adaptability; how to accept life as it is and to never look back with regret. Instead, Hummingbird shows us how to re-visit the past for the purpose of releasing it. She helps us to see that if we step aside, we may see our life differently.

*Adapted from various books and internet sources, including: *Animal Speak*, by Ted Andrews; *Totems*, by Brad Steiger; and *Power Animals*, by Steven D. Farmer.

To John,
whose unflagging love,
partnership, and innate decency sustain me.
"this is the wonder that's keeping the stars apart."

ACKNOWLEDGMENTS

The Caregiver's Compass evolved in form and focus over a period of three years, during which it was nudged, critiqued, and supported by numerous special people. Each helped me to keep going, arriving in my path when I most needed them.

First, I would like to thank Sydney Rice-Harrild for being the person who inspired me to take the step of writing professionally. She honors me with her wise coaching. She is a dear friend, a gift in my life. I am forever and profoundly grateful.

Deepest gratitude for my editor, Alice Whittelsey. Wordsmithing with my sister Alice was a joy. Her rigorous pursuit of best expression whittled my words down to their truest meaning. Her friendship is ever-present. This book is partly hers.

Fervent thanks to my relay team of experts, Elizabeth Whaley, Monique Raphel High, and Wendy Lazear. Each supported me at a critical stage of development. Liz first saw value in the memoir from which this book derived. She attended its birth, feeding me with seasoned feedback chapter by chapter. Then my agent Monique's belief in my work kept me moving forward. Finally, Wendy's immediate support of this book showed me that indeed, with perseverance, it would be published.

Profound gratitude to Alexis Teitz, my head cheerleader, for her constancy of friendship throughout caregiving and writing, and for modeling self-expression.

Thanks to the rest of my cheering squad: Pam Greene, for her big-hearted presence and gift of humor; Sarah Tilson, for helping me to "let my light shine" in spite of myself; Linda Cooper, for her enthusiasm about my work; Ann Hopkins, Paula Wall, Tish Lewis, Barbara Benham, Linda Hillier, and posthumously, Joann Lipshires, for their belief and encouragement; Rev. Kendra Ford for inviting me to co-write and preach our sermon on redemption, my first attempt to put this caregiving journey into words; John O'Leary, my brilliant personal coach; my readers for their excellent insights; my writing group who pored over these chapters, giving invaluable advice from so many perspectives; and my chorus, Voices from the Heart, for empowering radical self-expression. I felt the presence of each and all as I wrote.

With an eye to the past, I would like to acknowledge my mother, who gave me my love of words, and without whom this book would not have been written. With an eye to the future, I acknowledge the Eden Alternative for giving me a new vision of my future as part of the transformation of long-term care.

And first and last, deepest gratitude for my treasured life partner, John, for standing by me through it all, seeing my possibility, and making way for this book.

Contents

HOW TO USE THIS BOOK

The chemistry between adult children and their loved ones is determined by a myriad of factors, such as personalities, histories, and life circumstances. These factors go a long way to determining your caregiving style. Asking the useful questions about who you are, your relationships, and your ways of coping will open up an ever-clearer path. The answers you assert will influence all of your caregiving, determining where you set boundaries, telling you the actions or inactions that are appropriate for you, your family, and your loved one.

Since balanced effective caregiving depends on asking the right questions, each section of this book is followed by four journaling prompts or questions. You may be tempted to skip them, but they are here to deepen your experience. Responding to them will allow you to make the material your own by clarifying what will best serve you. Putting thoughts out on a page, seeing them verbalized in front of you, carries much more weight than simply running them through your mind. Record your responses in a caregiving journal that you keep with the book. Later, you will be able to refer back to what you have written to see how far you have come.

The following considerations will broaden your view of your unique circumstances, setting the stage for the Mindful Caregiving principles to make a difference in your caregiving experience.

WHAT IS A CAREGIVER?

I define a caregiver as anyone who cares deeply about the well-being of someone who is debilitated. Support can be offered long-distance or in person, part-time or full-time. The choice to be a caregiver will come to most of us, if it hasn't already. At some point, you might want to ask yourself, *What does caregiving mean to me?* It's not as though anyone prepares us for this role. Ask five people and you might hear that caregiving means:

Keeping your loved one physically safe and comfortable;
Supporting your loved one in aging however (s)he wants;
Caring for your loved one as perhaps (s)he once cared for you;
Making sure your loved one doesn't make any unsafe decisions; or
Maximizing your loved one's freedom as (s)he ages with dignity.

Your answer to this first fundamental question will guide you in the time to come. It will be the context of commitment from which everything else follows. It informs you as to what is important, telling you where to set your boundaries. It provides a beacon to keep you on track throughout your caregiving journey. Which of those five responses resonates most strongly for you? Or is there some other that you could put in your own words?

WHO ARE YOU?

Apart from your relationship with your loved one, what is your caregiving role—primary caregiver, long-distance supporter, family friend? Whatever your role, your emotional adjustments are real and complex.

The forces that determine how you react are, to a large extent, invisible. Even more telling than your caregiving role will be your personality, your habitual ways of being, and your family history. These have made your life work up to now with varying degrees of success. These factors directly impact your ability to cope during caregiving, either keeping you on course, or throwing you off course. Your success will be determined by your flexibility in the way you navigate caregiving. You will learn to tack. For instance:

Are you better at processing information than managing human relations? You might need to learn to think with your heart, to use your intuition;.

Are you a habitual nurturer? Caregiving will likely call on you to develop boundaries;

Are you automatically empathetic? You might need to take a stand in spite of that;

Is it often hard to fathom why people think and live as they do? Understanding of others' world views will make caregiving far easier.

With emotional intelligence and a few new thought tools, you will be able to chart your own course through this emotional time. Your new skills will keep you moving forward with greater ease. Throughout this book, you will practice how to be present, shift your communications, and welcome change in the three main areas of your caregiving: your emotions, your well-being, and your effectiveness.

INTRODUCTION - CHOSEN BY CAREGIVING

When "the call" comes, most people, regardless of gender or family history, feel an almost primal response. Some feel the urge to rise to the occasion of caregiving by supporting or fixing the situation. Some simply feel like running away. Most of us feel a combination of the above.

The decision to take on caregiving is not a simple one. This time of life, for most of us, is already complicated by managing children, careers, illness, divorce, and/or financial concerns. Underlying it all can be low-grade or chronic stress over the impermanence of life or family dysfunction. As we flip-flop between worries and a wish to do well, we can feel stuck by simultaneous feelings of approach and avoidance. Like the Push-mi-pull-yu in the children's book *Dr. Doolittle,* it can be hard to move forward.

The latest spiritual writings (by Ram Daas, Eckhart Tolle and others) tell us that to embrace life fully, we must attend to the present moment. That is never truer than in caregiving, yet it is no simple task. Discomfort makes life harder to embrace. So much is at stake; our loved one's health, our emotional balance, family relationships, perhaps our own health. Add to that conflicting feelings about caregiving, and the topic rapidly loses focus. We want to do a good job, but part of us wants to run for cover, a warm bed, or a stiff drink. Unfortunately the discomfort will still be there when we wake up. We deserve more than temporary relief. We need a way to proceed in greater peace.

A good deal of our discomfort comes from the fact that caregiving is a time of profound change. Indeed, life itself is change and it will change us. It can take a crisis to wake us up to the futility of resisting change. Mindful Caregiving tools will show you how to accept the inevitability of change, to roll with it and grow. You will increasingly see caregiving as a rich part of life. One of your goals could even be to provide caregiving as an act of choosing life. Yes, caregiving and life will change you, but you have some say as to how.

THE MINDFUL CAREGIVING ALTERNATIVE

Most family caregivers don't step into caregiving, we fall into it. Life happens. You can be sailing along under a fair wind, and suddenly you're responding to circumstances you never anticipated, capsizing emotionally, and wondering how to keep your head above water. Caregiving brings many mindless moments of reacting to circumstances. It can feel like concentrated living partly because the risks are more vital than in everyday life. They carry greater urgency, as you protect the life you have, while trying to prolong the life of your loved one.

Your alternative to falling victim to the emotions and events of caregiving is to step mindfully into it with self-awareness, meeting its challenges in a learning way. Jerry Lopper, a life skills coach, suggests, "Think of self-awareness as a feedback system, a way of seeing your behaviors, and even your thoughts, from the perspective of another, but with immediate feedback. Self-awareness allows for self regulation, correcting the thoughts, words, or deeds before they are completed, (allowing for) corrections whenever your thoughts, words, or behaviors stray from those that best serve whom you wish to be." Mindfulness also includes emotional awareness. Lopper tells us, "A person's emotions are fail-safe indicators of alignment with the authentic self and life purpose." Or in this case, your caregiving purpose.

The Caregiver's Compass is an emotional survival handbook for family caregivers. It contains thought tools and techniques for easing your way through the periodic turbulence of caregiving. You will navigate using life coaching wisdom to foster your own emotional resilience. Step-by-step you will optimize caregiving for both you and your loved one. Whether caregiving is an act of love or duty, or an attempt to redeem history, you will learn to visualize your best outcomes. You can afford to be optimistic.

Is it possible, then, to go beyond mere survival and thrive during caregiving?

Yes. Caregiving can enrich the rest of your life.

Challenges and opportunities are both larger than life and more fundamental. There is more at stake, but there is also more to gain. Like life, caregiving won't be what you think it will be. A relationship with a loved one can be made new. You can learn who your friends are and find your own voice. Hearts are tested, minds are challenged, relationships are stretched. Through it all, you can discover yourself. Now let's begin to explore your caregiving experience.

Part One
The Mindful Caregiving Principles

Be Present

Your present, the present moment, is the only point in time from which you can make choices and take action. If you are unaware or running on automatic, you miss opportunities to choose. Therefore, the first operating principle is to be present. We will look at specific techniques to help you be present so that you can clearly see the choices available to you as your caregiving unfolds.

Shift Communications

You create your experience of the present moment in the words that you think and speak, and in the way you listen. Your thoughts are the lens through which you see your caregiving. For better or worse, your words generate your experience. Your listening connects you to your world. The quality of your communications can stop you, or move you forward. Throughout this book, as you learn to think, speak and listen in new ways, you will see new possibilities for yourself and others. You and your relationships can be free to clarify and evolve.

Welcome Change

When steering your way through caregiving, as when steering a boat, you must maintain forward motion. As the caregiving captain, you will learn how to stay in motion and chart your course. Resistance to change will hold you back, while acceptance will make progress possible. Using this book, you will identify opportunities for acceptance that will free you to move forward.

CHAPTER ONE

BEING PRESENT

I have realized that the past and future
are really illusions, that they exist in the present,
which is what there is,
and all there is.
—Alan Watts, philosopher

Caregiving is life-changing. You can influence what that means, be the author of that change, but only to the degree that you can be present. In caregiving as in life, only in the present moment are you free to shift your speaking, shift your experience and embrace change. That's Mindful Caregiving in a nutshell. In fact nothing exists but the present moment. The future can call us forward but our response to that calling exists only in the present. The past shows up as positive or negative memories, depending on the meaning we attach to it, right here and now. The question is, on what will you focus? To what will you be present? What caregiving experience will you create?

This first chapter establishes the primary ground which makes possible the avenues of change presented in upcoming chapters. In this chapter you will learn three ways you can capitalize on the moment: by being present to possible choices, by being present to and managing your thoughts, and by being present to self-awareness.

Every choice moves us closer to
or farther away from something.
Where are your choices taking your life?
—Eric Allenbaugh, leadership consultant

BE PRESENT TO YOUR CHOICES

When choosing caregiving, the key word is choice. Fall haphazardly into caregiving, buffeted by memories, past-rooted emotions, and anxieties about the future, and you will have a rough trip. But consciously return yourself to the present moment, and many more choices become available. Be clear—it is your choice. Perhaps you will find it necessary to say no, especially if family history has been troubling. But if you say yes, say it freely.

At first glance, a free choice looks anything but easy. Many of us are already torn by a multitude of commitments and adjustments. Kids, grandkids, career, health issues, retirement, and more compound the situation. If you do choose it, how do you survive it with your lifestyle, relationships, and self intact? It can seem a narrow path that winds between helping someone in need, and preserving your own life. How can we talk about freedom in choosing caregiving when it feels so restrictive?

As throughout caregiving, it is normal to begin with more questions than answers. Useful questions point to real choices you can make now, while others only raise more unknowns, making the future still murkier. Questions like "How long will it last?" "Will it require years or even decades?" "How well will I cope?" can make the decision feel daunting due to the importance of the commitment and its lack of specificity.

Psychologist Dr. Karen Sherman tells us in her book, *Mindfulness and The Art of Choice*, "No doubt there will always be situations with which to contend—some are bumps, others feel more like a tornado. These are all part of life. The acceptance of that fact alone is very important because if you try to control everything, or at least be prepared for everything, you will always feel out of control."

So take a deep breath. Focus on the questions that can be answered immediately. Along the way you will make choices and more answers will come. Consciously and freely committing to caregiving will lessen your resistance and ease your discomfort -- and then the answers will follow. Like saying "I Do" in marriage, you can make your commitment, and later learn exactly how to fulfill that commitment. The energy you save by freely choosing you can then pour into learning from caregiving. The lessons will be a gift to yourself, as well as your loved one.

When you do ask questions, choose ones that will yield useful answers, such as:

- How close to this caregiving process should I be at first?
- How much of myself am I willing to give at the beginning?
- With what attitude will I take it on?
- What am I not willing to sacrifice?

When I was first considering what my life would be like with Mom in it, I asked myself *What is my goal?* Initially my answer was to help make Mom's life easier while protecting myself. From that answer flowed a series of choices and actions that set the stage for caregiving: frequency and length of visits; types of services rendered; various kinds of self-care. Over time, Mom's needs became clearer as I became less self-protective. My goal shifted to maximizing Mom's freedom and, whenever possible, preserving her dignity.

As you move forward, the more consciously you make your caregiving choices, the more alive and effective you will be. You can choose empowering or disempowering words to describe your experience. You can choose what you will make of what another person is saying or doing. You can choose whether you will or will not take action, how you take action, and what results will be acceptable.

In *The Mindful Brain*, Daniel Siegel tells us, "Instead of being on automatic and mindless, mindfulness helps us awaken, and by reflecting on the mind we are enabled to make choices, and thus change becomes possible." Much of your success will depend on where you focus your awareness. Focus on problems, and you will experience problems. Focus on challenges and opportunities, and you will have quite a different quality of experience. To get your bearings, start where you are by looking at the breadth of your life, your inner world as well as your outer circumstances. Start with the useful questions that reveal constructive choices. As we move through these chapters, I will show you how to shift your focus so as to gradually shift your experience. Then you will begin to generate the most useful answers.

The following journaling prompts will help you to engage with the choices available to you now. Make notes in your caregiving journal.

JOURNALING PROMPTS ON CHOICE

Turn to your caregiving journal and respond to the following:

1. What questions, for you, have the most urgency, regardless of how easily they can be answered? Make a list. List also the questions that crop up with the greatest frequency regardless of importance. Include all questions that come to mind.

2. Read through your list. Which questions are, for now at least, unanswerable? Put a "U" next to each, indicating that these are "Unanswerable." Your most useful choice is to think about these as little as possible.

3. What are all of the other questions that you have concerning caregiving? Many of these will point you toward a choice of action which you can note beside each. For instance, if the question is, "What kind of support will I need?" the actions you might choose could include: reflect on what would feel like support; search on-line for "support for caregivers" to see what others are saying; or call a friend or family member whom you trust to talk it over. Or let's say your question is, "How am I going to deal with my troublesome sister/brother?" Your choice could include: meet with a counselor or therapist to get your feelings sorted out and your priorities straight; decide to look for the most positive ways to think and feel about her/him; or decide at first to deal only with the people who are the least problematic. You can shelve some issues, and deal with them later.

4. What are other choices that you have been considering? List them. These could include choices of how to feel, whom to call, what to learn, how to speak, what to agree to, or what to ignore. Don't edit or self-correct—include everything however seemingly small. Notice on both of your lists which items are appropriately yours to handle, and which would be better dealt with by someone else. Put "Mine" next to those that are yours. For the others, write down the name of a different responsible person. From which questions are you willing to back off? Cross them off your lists.

Your innermost thoughts are beliefs
that unfold as your universe.
—Albert Einstein

BE PRESENT TO YOUR THOUGHTS

Daniel Siegel calls mindfulness "waking up from a life on automatic." How often do you have a flash of awareness of the automatic voice running inside your head? That voice seems to have a will of its own, a will that is not always in your best interest. Let's take a closer look at what that can mean to you during caregiving.

Most of us live as though life just shows up, and then we respond to it in thoughts, words, and actions. It feels as though life occurs outside of us, its impact on us providing our experience. Especially in caregiving, we live reactively. But you have more say over your present-moment experience than you think you do, or more accurately, as much as you think you do.

Consider this possibility: the meanings that you attach to caregiving in your thoughts actually generate your experience. If that were true, it would be crucial to your well-being to manage the meanings in your thoughts. But before you can shift the meaning, you must notice your thoughts as they happen in the present moment. In order to shift any way of thinking or acting, you must first be paying attention. Rather than automatically doing and saying things as you always have, be first and foremost an observer. Think of your life as the mirror of your thoughts. Listen to the words with which you describe your life, then watch your life show up in alignment with them. Notice how you feel when you think, *Caregiving will be hard*. Notice the shift in your feelings when you think, *Caregiving will be a challenge*. Your thoughts and your self-talk in each present moment are, to a large extent, generating your life experience.

USA Swimming, the governing body for the sport of swimming in the U.S., recognizes the impact of self-talk on effectiveness. In their Mental Toolbox article called *Learning to be Your Own Best Friend*, they identify five types of self-talk that can undermine performance: focusing on the past or future, weaknesses, outcomes, and uncontrollable factors; and demanding perfection.

That might well have been written for caregivers. In the "game" of life we make up our experience of past, present and future in the way that we are thinking... right now. You are making up the way you experience these words in the way that you are thinking about them right now. Shift the words you use to think about a thing, and new possibilities present themselves. Partway through my caregiving time, I had an experience that made this principle dramatically and wonderfully clear.

When Mom moved to the nursing home, more people entered her life, most of them aides. They were buzzing in and out, helping her to dress, bringing her meals. Many were faceless to me, as their shifts did not coincide with my visiting schedule. It didn't take me long to notice that "they" were in the habit of dropping Mom's laundry on the floor of her closet, rather than putting it in the laundry bag.

I began to simmer. Internally I railed against their slovenly behavior. I almost felt that they had it in for me. After a couple of weeks of this it occurred to me to take a little inventory of my emotional state. I weighed my lost sleep and wasted energy against the relatively lesser importance of the laundry. I knew that something had to change. My first thought was that "they" had to change, but how could I communicate that? I felt I was in a bind, since I depended on their good will to help make Mom's life more pleasant. I also had no idea who "they" were. Suddenly it occurred to me that maybe "they" weren't the problem.

I had been making hasty assumptions about them. The frustration was my own—I could change my part of this equation. I reconsidered. People who work in nursing homes don't do it for the money, they do it because they care about people. They lead busy, fractured lives, constantly responding to requests and demands. Perhaps I could make their lives easier, and my own. I installed a large plastic container in the closet that took up most of the floor space. It would be hard to miss. I put on it a sign saying, "Thank You For Putting Laundry In Here" with a big colorful smiley face, and signed it. The problem went away. The lessons I took from this were: first, to listen to the words I use to describe others and their motivations; second, to take responsibility for my own feelings; and third, to enact the simplest solution.

The next time you feel like a victim to circumstances, or find yourself fuming about the ineptitude of others, take a look at your thoughts. As Oprah says in her introduction to Marianne Williamson's *Miracle Thought* podcasts, "Have you ever asked, 'What am I thinking?' Best question you could ask." And it is.

We'll be taking a much deeper cut at this principle of self-talk. You will learn how to wield it as a powerful tool for creating your caregiving experience. For now, begin your exploration by responding to the following journaling prompts.

JOURNALING PROMPTS ON THOUGHTS

Turn to your caregiving journal and respond to the following:

1. What do you believe is true about caregiving? Do you think of it as hard, inspiring, tragic, or galvanizing? What do you tell others about what you are doing? What are your preconceptions? Your assumptions? What is your tone of voice when talking about caregiving. Write down whatever comes to mind.

2. Which of these are interpretations that you are prepared to stand behind? Are they beliefs that you would free-heartedly choose to actualize in the way that you live and speak? Are there modifications you could make to them to have them support you better? Instead of "hard" could you say "challenging"? "Tragic" might become "a mixed bag emotionally." Write a revision of your beliefs that will better serve you and everyone involved.

3. What are the domains of your life—your relationships, your commitments, the things that matter to you? These could include marriage, community, children, and work. Make a list. Check within. How do you feel about each one? Do you see trouble anywhere? Write next to each the words you use to describe those aspects of your life. Then write next to each some different descriptive words that you could use that would shift your experience. The more you can fine tune your experience of all of your life, the easier it will be to shift your caregiving experience.

4. How much time do you spend thinking about the past or the future? Write down a few of the things you think about. Which thoughts serve you in the present? For the ones that don't serve you, write down a rephrasing that feels more constructive. Circle which thoughts you could put aside in favor of being present to your life right now.

People avoid change until the pain
of remaining the same is greater
than the pain of changing.
—Unknown

BE PRESENT TO SELF-LEARNING

The early days and weeks of caregiving require coping with many details as you nail down the logistics of living. When the major elements have been handled, permit yourself to slow down to let your emotions catch up. Allow an ebb and flow between practical control and expressive release. By riding life's current you learn resilience that will buoy and empower you to manage future details. At this early stage of your learning process, a few simple principles will help you to stay on course.

Early in life we learned behaviors in response to our parents. Throughout life these behaviors have determined how you navigate. Some have become your strategies for survival. When caregiving gets turbulent, your first responses will be habitual.

Initially these behaviors help you stay balanced, though not yet resilient. These long-held behaviors feel safe, but at some point familiar ways of operating can stop working. As Sydney Rice-Harrild tells us in her book *Choice Points*, "We all have an internal system for producing results that operates on its own, helping us to produce consistent results without our even having to think about it, but it doesn't work in our favor when what we want is managed change." Study your survival strategies so that you will later be able to adapt when they don't work. Do you take charge, telling others what to do? That may not always be appropriate. Do you isolate yourself to get your bearings? There might not always be time for that. What will you do when caregiving calls on you to respond in a new way?

Consider the workplace proverb about the boiled frog. If you put a frog into boiling water, it will jump out. But if you put it in cool water and slowly heat it, the frog won't jump—it will die. Like frogs, we can refuse to notice when the water we swim in has changed. We are willing to stay with the familiar rather than jump. Look for opportunities to jump.

When I first entered caregiving, I packed a well-stocked survival kit. I had monumental patience. I tackled life in order to subdue it, to make it safe. I knew how to listen intently and watch carefully. I was good-humored, reflective, and proactive, but let's face it, I was a control hound. That skill had kept me safe as a kid, and made me a respected, productive adult. But now too much energy was being wasted controlling circumstances. When Mom gained weight, I pressured her to exercise. I lectured the nursing home staff on diet, quizzed the aides about snacks. Despite good intentions, I was insufferable. As I tried to muscle life into submission, the staff began to avoid me. My mother stiffened when I entered the room. Life called for a new way—not just new actions but a new way of being, of relating to the whole situation.

As a life coach, I knew that a good deal of life's pain comes from resisting. I knew I would need to release some control to gain greater emotional resilience. I looked for opportunities to listen to my intuition. Rather than charging in with logical action, I began to intuit how to change course. I questioned my automatic assumptions such as *It's my job to protect my mother.* One day Mom's college roommate called and told me point blank to back off from helping my mother too much. She said I should live my own life. The day after the conversation, my voice with Mom had shifted. I was direct, candid about the realities of her situation. She responded well. The next day she said, "You get so used to people doing things for you, you forget you can do things yourself." And then she opened the door for me to push the wheelchair through. Her self-sufficiency became one of my new goals.

It is one thing to jump into the river, quite another to relax in the current. When we see that we are part of something much bigger, we become able to respond appropriately. My emerging intuition saved Mom's life a time or two. Seeing that I was part of the health care system, I relaxed into following my intuition. Rather than trying to control all aspects of Mom's caregiving, I focused on my necessary and appropriate contributions.

I opened myself to change, freeing myself to ask new questions. Questions shifted my experience. What might my mother want to recollect about her life? What aspects of my childhood could she illuminate? What medical information could I learn to feel more empowered? My definition of personal growth became "Expanding who I am so as to eliminate obstacles to my fullest experience of life."

To gain resilience, become a student of your survival strategies. Then listen for intuitions offering new ways of coping. The lessons in caregiving are preparing you for the future. Later, when you look back, it may almost seem as though a plan were unfolding. Your intuition will have been your trusted guide.

Now take a moment to journal about self-learning, who you have been, and who you would like to be.

JOURNALING PROMPTS ON SELF-LEARNING

Turn to your caregiving journal and respond to the following:

1. What are your greatest personality strengths? What traits define your character? Which have gotten you through life's ups and downs? Forthrightness? Listening? Playfulness? Problem-solving? Which ones have you inherited from someone else? Make a list along with any notes that seem relevant. If you want some ideas of traits, a search on the internet for "personality traits" will turn up long complete lists from which to draw.

2. Which of these traits have helped you to navigate challenges in the past? Make a note by these. Also note the ones you default to under stress. These would be your front line reaction to a crisis. Others you have developed to help you get through in the long run. Add any other traits that come to mind.

3. Which of these traits might not be so useful in caregiving? If a trait would be useful in one situation but not another, write down the kinds of situations. Where are the limits of your traits' usefulness? When could it be a handicap to be authoritative? When might you want to shift from being playful to taking care of business, or vice versa?

4. What new skill or awareness could caregiving require? Write other strengths or ways of navigating that you would like to learn. What does your intuition tell you when you think of the categories of challenges ahead of you? Also note the potentially necessary skills that you do not have, and have no interest in learning. Who might you call on who does have those skills or traits? With whom could you partner? Write down their names.

In this chapter we have covered the first principle, that of being present. We have seen that, once present, you have the opportunity to see the choices that you otherwise would have missed, like deciding what caregiving will mean for you and your lifestyle. We have considered the power of being present to your thoughts, noticing the reality they are creating for you. We have looked at being present to what you can learn about yourself, your character traits, your survival strategies. Below are some resources for your continued exploration.

In the next chapter, Shift Your Communications, we'll discover the leverage available to you in the way that you communicate. This means not only the way you speak to yourself and to others, it means the way that you choose to listen. Attention to your speaking and listening can give you far greater control over how easily your caregiving unfolds.

RESOURCES

Books

Arriving at Your Own Door: 108 Lessons in Mindfulness, by Jon Kabat-zinn

Mindfulness and The Art of Choice: Transform Your Life, by Karen H. Sherman

The Mindful Brain: Reflection and Attunement in the Cultivation of Well-Being, by Daniel J. Siegel

The Power of Now: A Guide to Spiritual Enlightenment by Eckhart Tolle

Full Catastrophe Living: How to Cope with Stress, Pain and Illness Using Mindfulness Meditation, by Jon Kabat-Zinn and Joan Borysenko

Websites & Blogs

The Center for Contemplative Mind in Society www.contemplativemind.org

Contemplative Psychotherapy www.contemplativepsychotherapy.net

Self-awareness Suite 101 articles www.self-awareness.suite101.com

The Institute for Mindfulness Studies www.instituteformindfulnessstudies.com

Wildmind www.wildmind.org

Embracing change Blog www.embracingchangeaward.blogspot.com

CHAPTER TWO

SHIFTING YOUR COMMUNICATIONS

Be careful of your thoughts;
they may become words at any moment.
—Ira Gassen

As you become more aware of your present moment, what you *do* with that moment becomes paramount. Your most powerful leverage point for creating a good caregiving experience is in your communications. The words you think and speak can open a new way forward for you and your loved one. However, they can just as easily generate obstacles to your well-being.

Even more powerful than speaking and thinking is the quality of your listening, which can open up or shut down your relationships. Maintaining relationships is an essential skill during caregiving.

These principles are simple, yet at first can be tricky to grasp. Let's take a closer look at how you can make them work for your caregiving advantage. In this chapter we will explore how you can generate a more empowering reality in your thinking, how your speaking can influence the way your life moves, and how you can improve your relationships with your listening.

You either believe what you think,
Or you question it.
There is no other choice.
- Byron Katie

SHIFT YOUR THINKING

Simple life data, the things you know with complete certainty, are merely facts. These facts are unadorned by interpretation. They have not yet been run through the filters of feelings and meanings. "The chair sits beside the door." "My mother came into the room." However, what we call *our* truth, our reality, is uniquely personal and far from simple. Reporters at crime scenes frequently find onlookers who view the same incident yet tell different stories. Two siblings growing up in the same family can describe two quite different personal realities.

What we call our reality is more accurately the stories that we weave to explain life. It is our interpretation of events, our embroidering of meaning, that embellishes the simple facts of life. For example, let's say you observe a family member entering the room you are in and turning to look out the window. What you feel about that will be caused by your thoughts, such as, *She strode angrily into the room and didn't even say hello! What did I do?* Your emotional experience is driven by your story *about* what happened. You might just as well have thought, *I wonder what she has on her mind? She's distracted—it must be important.*

Usually our minds run on automatic, collapsing this distinction between the facts of what *is* and the story we tell to explain them. Very little in our minds is absolute truth. You can trust your mind to spin off facts about as much as you can trust the TV newscast to give pure information. When we lack information about what is happening for someone else, we rush to fill the void with our own imaginings. If we don't know another person's intentions or feelings, we launch into spinning our own surmisings.

Rather than automatically deciding that a thought is a hard and fast truth, you can begin to question the underpinnings of it. Byron Katie is an inspiring teacher whose mission is to show people how to end their own suffering. She leads people through an exercise, a process of inquiry, that shifts the way they see what is troubling them. Katie has people identify and verbalize what they are telling themselves is true, such as, "Nobody loves me" or "I'll never be a success." Then she has them ask themselves questions such as, *Is that thought true? Absolutely true? What happens when I think that thought? Who would I be without that thought? Could another thought be more true? Perhaps the inverse of that thought? Do my thoughts hide me from life?* By the time you get through Katie's line of questioning you learn that there is always a host of possible ways of thinking about a thing or problem. Often the alternatives are far more life-serving.

So this is good news. You make your own meaning. You can alter your experience of caregiving, your past, or your future, by noticing your thoughts in the moment, and being responsible for the reality they are creating.

Jon Kabat-Zinn tells us, "How we see things affects how much energy we have for doing things, and our choices about where to channel what energy we do have." How we see things is determined by the thoughts we think. As you learn consciously to weave your experience, you will feel less at the mercy of life and those around you. As you broaden the interpretive lens through which you see, you re-tune your inner climate. You eliminate obstacles to fully experiencing your life, increasing your capacity for being fully alive (and effective) in all stages of caregiving and all aspects of life.

Take a moment to write in your journal about the ways that you think.

JOURNALING PROMPTS ON SHIFTING THINKING

Turn to your caregiving journal and respond to the following:

1. Write out a detailed personal description of your experience of caregiving. Everything about it. Then read it through slowly, asking yourself, *Do the words I have chosen support me in doing my best caregiving?* Note any insights.

2. Which parts of your description are absolute fact and truth? Highlight them. Notice what is left, how much of your story of caregiving is open to interpretation.

3. Did you ever have a relationship that was damaged because of your need to be right? Write about it. Also write down a time when your ability to have an open interpretation of a person, their words or their actions, made life easier. What have been the benefits to you when you have held a flexible interpretation of a person or situation?

4. Who might be swaying your view of your life? Whose reality do you buy into without question? Write down some other possible interpretations of your reality.

If we worked on the assumption that
what is accepted as true really is true,
then there would be little hope for advancement.
- Orville Wright

SHIFT YOUR SPEAKING

If your mother ever said to you, "WATCH your language!" she had no idea of the power of her command. When we speak we create realities both for ourselves and for those around us. We are constantly and unwittingly being infected by others, and we infect others with our own realities. Just watch the news on TV, and see how you feel afterward. Or imagine yourself visiting your loved one in the hospital. You are walking down the hallway when you overhear two people talking. One of them points at a nurse coming down the hall, and tells her friend, "That one has a lousy attitude." Later, you meet that nurse in your loved one's room. Do you feel good about her caring for your loved one? What are the assumptions with which you greet her? How do you know they are "real"?

Now imagine the impact of your own speaking as you converse or "share" with your siblings or your loved one. The words we choose elicit a particular response. They are like an invitation to have someone join in a particular conversation, to see things as we do. Perhaps you have a friend who is prone to saying things like, "I'm having the most horrible day!" or "You won't believe what she said to me!" By one way of thinking, you are being invited to join in awfulizing or gossiping. While these forms of communication in ordinary life can be seen as recreational, (commonly called "sharing") caregiving is not ordinary life. Your energy and attitude are to be safeguarded at all cost. How do you feel when someone tries to draw you in with recreational whining? How do you feel when you yourself begin a litany about how horrible life is? Horrible? Of course there can be times when you need to unload, but use them carefully. Set yourself a time limit. Then shift into constructive forms of communication that are sourced by your commitment to caregiving. When you say "Caregiving is hard" do you mean you are committed to it being hard? How does your feeling about it shift when you say "Caregiving is a challenge"?

Carlos Fernando Flores Labra is a Chilean entrepreneur and former cabinet minister under President Salvador Allende. He spent three years as a political prisoner after the military coup of General Augusto Pinochet (1973-1976). He knew the power of language. During those three years, the way he chose to think and speak gave him his freedom. He said, "I never told a victim story about my imprisonment. Instead, I told a transformation story - about how prison changed my outlook, about how I saw that communication, truth, and trust are at the heart of power. I made my own assessment of my life, and I began to live it. That was freedom."

We're all like fish swimming in a communal fish bowl. Both our own words and those spoken by others define our experience. When I was diagnosed with colon cancer five years into caregiving, I recognized how true this was. I was suddenly hypersensitive to people who in any way promoted useless drama in their speaking. I wrote in my diary:

> *I have little experience with feminine compassion, and don't quite know what to do with it. Some of it's draining. Some isn't. Some women friends seem to love the drama, the negative story of illness. It feels as though they're too eager to climb inside my experience. I need to distance myself to be able to discover or create my own experience. Some others are able to support me by being more positive, by not climbing into bed with me.*

Perhaps you can think of someone you know who speaks in a way that deflates you or drains your energy. When someone is being negative or hyper-critical, I've been known to say, "Hey! Stop pooping in the fish bowl."

So, since your words generate your present reality for you, and also affect those to whom you speak, you may want to pay attention to the words coming out of your mouth. One of your mantras for caregiving could be, *If I'm going to make something up, make it good.*

Take a few moments to document in your journal some of the words with which you have been generating your experience of caregiving, noticing alternatives that could better serve you.

JOURNALING PROMPTS ON SHIFTING SPEAKING

Turn to your caregiving journal and respond to the following:

1. What was a recent meaningful conversation in which you were talking about something important to you, but the conversation just didn't feel as good as you would have liked? It could have been with a family member, a health professional, or a good friend. What were the words you remember using to describe that thing that was important to you?

2. Underline the operative words that define or give rise to your emotions in relation to the experience. "I am so angry!" "Caregiving is too hard." "She's losing her mind." "You don't care." Are your statements absolutely true? Do you stand behind them? Do you freely choose that way of seeing things? Journal a bit about what you see. Might your words be diminishing your sense of control?

3. Exactly how do you think your way of speaking may have impacted the person to whom you were speaking? How did they impact you?

4. How did the words you used affect the outcome of the interaction, if any? Did anything result? If you can think of a different best possible outcome, what would it be? What words would have supported that best outcome?

To listen fully means to pay close attention
to what is being said beneath the words.
You listen not only to the 'music,'
but to the essence of the person speaking.
—Peter Senge

SHIFT YOUR LISTENING

"Real connections can't happen without effective listening," says Beverly Edgehill, president and chief executive of Partnership Inc. "I do think good listening is more complex than we perceive it to be," she says. "Listening is more than hearing."

Early in my caregiving decade, I tried to get one friend to listen to me. I said, "I really need to talk to you for just a bit." As she kept buzzing around the kitchen, cleaning up this and that, she said, "Go right ahead. I'm listening." I said, "No, I really need your attention. This is important." She replied, "That's fine. I can do two things at once. Go ahead." "No!" I said, "I need you to come into the living room, and sit down with me, and pay attention to what I'm going to say." Her response? "Oh, okay. Let me just find my cell phone, in case I get a call." Finally I blurted out, "No! No blasted cell phone! This is important!" My vehemence got her attention. When we were seated in the formal living room, I said, "I'm heading into a challenging time with my mom. I knew it would be when I chose it, but I'm really scared because I know it's going to change me." And my friend listened.

Listening is no passive state. We are never merely hearing someone else speaking. The *way* you are listening changes the way someone else *feels heard*. Not tending to your listening can be an easy way to damage a relationship. The quality of your listening influences the way someone else interprets you, which can change the direction of a conversation.

Your listening also limits and colors what you hear and believe. What you listen *for* is a filter, limiting what you let in. It is the context that creates the meaning, for you, in what someone else is saying. Whether or not we are aware of it, we are always actively listening *for* something. We may be listening for someone to be critical. We may be listening for their motives, or their message. Or we may simply be listening for entertainment. Your personality type is a major determiner of *what* you automatically listen for, and we will go into that later in greater depth. Here we'll just address the idea that you can choose the quality of your listening.

Your experience of another person has everything to do with the meanings that you add to what they say. And the meanings you add to what they say are slanted by what you are listening *for*. As an experiment, try listening for a learning opportunity. Listening for what you can learn (about the person, the topic, or yourself) can completely shift the energy and outcome of a conversation, allowing it to blossom in surprising ways.

For instance, let's say you are caregiving for your mother, who is a chronically dissatisfied person. You enter her room one day, and she begins complaining, "That aide intentionally left my walker just out of reach!" You might chalk it off to her bad attitude, if that is what you were expecting. Or you could ask yourself what the underlying message might be. Could it be that she is feeling her lack of control over her life? You test this theory by giving her a manual puzzle that you know she can solve, and her attitude immediately shifts. Finally she has something she can Do.

The way you listen can also shift the way another person feels about you. You can enter a difficult conversation, and then move it onto constructive ground by cultivating a non-judgmental, compassionate, or learning listening style. Ask yourself,

- What must it be like to live in their world?
- How would it feel to have their personality?
- What might have happened to them to have them speaking as they are?

"I pride myself on being able to multi-task. Does it cause me to be a good listener? Maybe not," says Edgehill. Too often, we rush to finish a conversation, to get the results *we* want, to get on to the next thing. Society gears us toward quick communications. Our listening cannot keep pace. If you move too fast through caregiving you may miss something important. You may lose an opportunity to let your loved one feel heard. You may miss your loved one's vague reference to a serious concern. You may overlook a chance to foster the mutual trust of your healthcare team.

"Life is short so you have to move slowly," an old Thai proverb tells us. Move slowly in your listening. Slowly listen beyond anger. Slowly listen without judgment. Slowly listen for opportunities for learning and connection.

Now answer the following questions in your journal about the ways that you listen, what you listen for, and what you could be listening for.

JOURNALING PROMPTS ON SHIFTING LISTENING

Turn to your caregiving journal and respond to the following:

1. List the key people in your caregiving experience, and beside each list what you listen *for* when you talk to them. What do you automatically expect from them? Support? Bossiness? Good humor? Judgement? What do you think you already know about each one's attitude or intention?

2. Think back to the past week for three conversations in which the way you were listening influenced what you were hearing in a less-than-useful way. In what other way could you have listened to each? How could a change in your listening have influenced the outcomes of your conversations?

3. If you were to practice listening in order to learn something, who could you listen to in this way to have a new experience of them? What might you learn?

4. During your conversations in the coming days, play with adopting various ways of listening to others. Listen for new qualities in them. Listen with appreciation for the differences between you. Journal about the resulting shifts in you and in them.

In this chapter, we discussed how to think your way to a more empowering reality. You saw that what happens in caregiving can be caused by the way that you speak. And you learned how to improve relationships by intentionally choosing a productive way of listening to others. In the next chapter, we will explore ways to move with the changes of caregiving so that you feel both freer and more balanced.

Resources About Communication

Books

Change Your Thoughts - Change Your Life: Living the Wisdom of the Tao by Dr. Wayne W. Dyer

Loving What is: How Four Questions Can Change Your Life
by Byron Katie and Stephen Mitchell

Self Talk, Soul Talk: What to Say When You Talk to Yourself
by Jennifer Rothschild, Robin McGraw

Finding Your Voice: A Woman's Guide to Using Self-Talk for Fulfilling Relationships, Work, and Life by Dorothy Cantor, Carol Goodheart, Sandra Haber, and Ellen McGrath

Language in Thought and Action: Fifth Edition by S.I. Hayakawa, Alan R. Hayakawa

Difficult Conversations: How to Discuss what Matters Most
by Douglas Stone, Bruce Patton, Sheila Heen, Roger Fisher

Are You Really Listening?: Keys to Successful Communication
by Paul J., Ph.D. Donoghue, Mary E. Siegel

Wisdom of Listening by Mark Brady

Websites

Interpersonal Communication www.abacon.com

Self Talk www.extension.org

Effective Interpersonal Communication www.humanresources.about.com

Exploring Non-verbal Communication www.nonverbal.ucsc.edu

Nonverbal Communication Skills www.helpguide.org

CHAPTER THREE

WELCOMING CHANGE

Without accepting the fact that everything changes,
we cannot find perfect composure.
Because we cannot accept the truth of transience,
we suffer.
—Shunryu Suzuki, Zen Master

Life is change—it will change us. If you have siblings, your relationship with them will probably change during caregiving. If you have a life partner, your relationship with him or her may also change. Certainly, if your loved one is aging, you are likely to witness dramatic changes. For most of us it is the unknown property of change that is unnerving, even though some of the changes may turn out to be quite positive. In caregiving, as in life, resisting change doesn't work well. Life gets seriously more painful. If you proceed mindfully and creatively while aligning with life, the changes can be for the better.

In this chapter you will learn how to shift to a less fearful state of mind, one in which you can begin to move with change and even welcome it. We will look at how to use questions to open yourself to new possibilities, how to identify what you are resisting and then respond differently, and how to feel greater freedom by approaching each moment as a learning opportunity.

The voyage of discovery lies
not in finding new landscapes
but in having new eyes.
—Marcel Proust

THE POWER OF QUESTIONING

While questioning your thinking can eliminate obstacles to your well-being, questioning aspects of your circumstances can reveal new opportunities for forward movement. If you approach challenging moments as learning opportunities, as a chance to see differently, you can stay in motion as you grow with the changes.

The website QuestionsForLiving.com is rooted in the premise that the quality of one's life is determined by the quality of one's questions. The site is an active research project based on that philosophy. The site provides questions that help you to "think critically about the questions that you should be asking [in order] to create an experience closely aligned with your hopes and expectations."

What might that mean for you as a student to caregiving? Let's say that you are caregiving for someone who has been in your life for a long time—a parent, a sibling, or a life partner—and their new behaviors are presenting a challenge. You might inquire into the connection between who (s)he has been and who you now are. For better or worse, this person may have been a role model for you, shared your life or even given you life. (S)he may have tried to instill in you behaviors and beliefs that were thought to be valuable. Some that you unconsciously absorbed may have served you well (or not.) Others you consciously chose to accept. They have served you well (or not.) You may have rebelled against still others, developing reactive habits of your own devising. Who we are is likely to be directly or indirectly informed by who our loved ones have been. Even the most challenging of histories teaches valuable living skills. Mundane aspects of life are fertile ground for inquiry, offering us clues to these inheritances.

In my diary I wrote about what I learned from clutter:

Yesterday Mom's fear undid her. This amorphous fear has no object, so she latches onto every concrete complaint in her path. This time it was clutter—she wanted it gone. I left with boxes piled high on a cart. In my garage the piles of boxes of her life keep getting higher.

I could see that when her emotional clutter was too much, attacking the physical clutter in her life helped her to feel in control. I reflected on the differences between her behaviors and my own:

Could my clutter be limiting me? Am I just a fearful person posing as someone of substance? Clutter tells me that I am of use. I make things happen. Do I look busy while staying safe, as in no movement? If I cleaned out my unused stuff, might something new happen? Movement is freedom. Freedom, that's scary—I might get the life I want? But I'd have to give up the comfort of hiding behind old habits. I hide behind clutter of my history's construction. Beyond those habits is my life, waiting to be lived.

You may have heard the Buddhist saying, "When the student is ready the teacher will appear." Caregiving can be that teacher, if you will choose to approach it as the student. What will follow will be a series of learning moments.

You may be spending more time with your loved one than you have in decades. This time won't come again. Asking questions now can yield gold. Reflect on the behaviors of your loved ones. They may have you wondering, *How did they come to be who they now are? Who were their role models?* Notice and explore the differences between you. Ask yourself, *How do we see life differently? Are our values different, or even at odds? How is life different now from what it has ever been?* Like unraveling a tangled ball of yarn, you can tease out learnings that will be of great value to you over the coming months.

Now engage with the following questions to begin exploring new paths of inquiry.

JOURNALING PROMPTS ON QUESTIONING

Turn to your caregiving journal and respond to the following:

1. Make a list of any unresolved disturbance you may be feeling about caregiving, people in your life, or your loved one's behavior. What irks you, distresses you, or makes you uneasy?

2. What are some new questions you could ask yourself about each bit of trouble? Do some have historical roots worth looking at? How might you look at each in a new way? What are the opportunities present in each?

3. Another fruitful inquiry is in the realm of values and beliefs. What are the life truths of your loved one? On what values and beliefs have they based their choices? Do you share these, or hold other views? How could you edit their beliefs to make them ones to which you could subscribe?

4. How are your loved one's values and beliefs consistent with the way (s)he is aging? How do your own values and beliefs influence the way you are responding to their aging and to caregiving?

What you resist persists.
—Carl Jung

THE POWER OF ALLOWING

"What you resist persists." What does that mean? A correlate to that is "What you focus on is what you get." Change your focus, change your life. Focus on (or resist) another's annoying behaviors, and you see only annoying behaviors. But focus on their wonderfulness and watch them get so much better! Allow others to be who they are and they improve.

There comes a time in caregiving when you may recognize how much of your energy is going into resisting—resisting life's changes, your loved one's aging or changing. You may resist the behavior of a sibling or partner, or a recent crisis. You could resist parenting your loved one. Beneath each resistance is a snippet of grief waiting to be named. And with resistance can come the urge to Do Something, to do anything, or to fix something or someone. When we find ourselves groping for an action to take, it can be that the only right action is inaction. Stop. Take a breath. Notice what is. You can't get beyond resistance until you clearly see it.

Five years into my mom's decade of decline, she decided to move out of her retirement community and into her own apartment. She was busting out because she didn't like living with old people. Much as I resisted her plan, I had to admire her spunk. Then five days before her move, she broke her ankle. While Mom struggled in rehab to regain lost ground, my sister and I completed the move. Three long months later Mom was sprung from rehab feeling giddy with the freedom of living in her own bright apartment. I charged around trying to enforce normalcy. Then I stopped long enough to take in what was *really* happening. The last three months had taken a toll. I wrote in my diary:

> *Mom is dithery today. Her words spill softly from her mouth. Thoughts float away, dissolving right there in mid-sentence. She sits lower than usual in her big brown recliner. The permeating dank of the April day has her crawling inside herself. Layers of life warm her like the flannel of the robe she's still wearing, though it is afternoon. She speaks in a childlike way, saying, "I need help. I need to talk things over." Though always anxious, she is rarely this directly needy.*

In caregiving, the only way out is through. Life isn't run by computer software—it doesn't have an "undo" command. I couldn't edit the facts of the present. Rather than pretending life was normal, I had to admit the truth; that Mom was less capable of independence than she had been three months before. I needed to accept circumstances exactly as they were.

As the serenity prayer suggests, for peace of mind you must accept the things you cannot change, change the things you can, and be aware of the difference. Part Two of this book addresses how to change what you can. For now, begin by identifying what you resist. Give each resistance a name. Know its nature. Some things are not yours to change. Sometimes a useful caregiving mantra can be "Not my business" or "Not my problem" or "Not mine to solve." Allowing circumstances to be as they are doesn't mean that you are choosing to *keep* them that way. By accepting and allowing, life is freed to evolve. Step two is identify what *must* happen now. When you look resistance in the face, and accept the change that is underway, you can distinguish what is truly important. Priorities reconfigure. You have cleared the way to see what is missing. Your actions or inactions, flowing from your new awareness, become appropriate to the situation at hand. The way you are being has aligned with reality. I wrote in my diary:

> *Mom's spirit seems so small. I switch gears and make mental trade-offs—I note what can wait and what truly needs doing. She and I pull her thoughts together, putting band aids on the fraying bits, slowly rebuilding her life to make it more whole. She needs to know that she has done a good job, that her life has mattered.*

Google "practicing acceptance" and you find: "Acceptance is feminine in nature; it implies receptivity... To practice acceptance is to embrace possibility and to allow space for further growth and deeper understanding." If you could allow caregiving to be what it is, how much easier might all of your life become? The self-defense discipline, Aikido, teaches us that when a force is moving toward us, if we counter that force head-on we could get hurt. But if we begin to move in the same direction as the force, we instantly gain some control and can redirect the power of that force. We become powerful in our ability to dance with adversity. Practice the allowance that will let you move *with* caregiving as you align with the force of life.

Answer the following questions about your resistance, and you will move yourself toward allowing, a much more comfortable way to be.

JOURNALING PROMPTS ON ALLOWING

Turn to your caregiving journal and respond to the following:

1. What do you resist in life, in your loved one, in someone else and/or in yourself? What do you not want in your life right now, and/or in your caregiving? What are you tired of trying to change?

2. What is your automatic way of responding when you are resisting? What do you think, feel, or do?

3. Make some notes here, exploring alternatives to the way you think about these things. What response would be more in tune with the way life is unfolding? What issues are truly important? Which could you begin to accept?

4. How has your world been changed by focusing on what you resist? With respect to that resistance, might you simply refocus on something more constructive? Like what? The more you can weed out moments of resistance, the more energy you will have to devote to what is important.

It isn't until we make that
'intuitive' connection in our brains
that real learning takes place.
—Mary Timme

THE POWER OF LEARNING

We have spoken of the power of asking useful questions so as to grow and move with change. We have looked at the energy gained by eliminating opportunities for resistance, thus allowing change. Now let's look at how your right brain can be an ally in learning, broadening your vision to help you welcome change.

The Psychology Encyclopedia tells us that, "While the left brain hemisphere is dominant in the areas of language and logic, the right-brain hemisphere is the center of nonverbal, intuitive, holistic modes of thinking." Left brain logic generates fairly linear answers to life. Right brain offers intuitive learning. As youngsters we are taught left-brain problem-solving and are rated in our use of it, while our ability to explore intuitive solutions is given short shrift. But when we're presented with chaotic times like caregiving, our left brain can only take us so far. When life isn't going the way we think it should, we immediately jump to left brain thinking to fix it. Left brain looks for facts, data, and if it can't find any, we worry, generating anxiety, frustration, fear, and judgments. Then our left brain looks for evidence to support the worry.

When we have access to facts and data, our left brain works well. But little in our lives is data-based. When dealing with an emotional situation or with a story we have invented about what is true in our lives, the left brain is no help.

Creativity lives in the right brain where we reflect, imagine, reinterpret, and see new possibilities. This is where we make learning leaps. The power of questioning that we discussed earlier lives in the right brain. Imagine that you are engulfed by an apparent crisis. You enmesh yourself in trouble by saying "I worry about..." But switch your response to "I wonder about..." and suddenly you are under way. You feel the shift in your body. It is a lightening, an opening rather than a closing down. In that little moment of switching to a state of wonder, you have moved your thinking from the left brain to the right brain, where new solutions become possible through new ways of thinking. The following diagram, adapted from Stephen Carr Associates' work, clarifies how this happens.

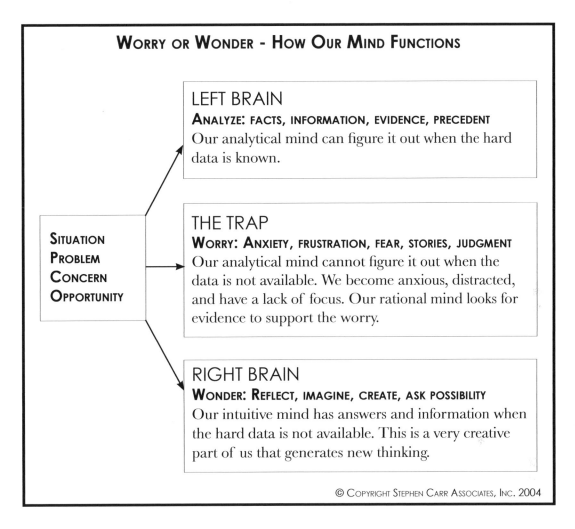

WORRY OR WONDER - HOW OUR MIND FUNCTIONS

SITUATION
PROBLEM
CONCERN
OPPORTUNITY

LEFT BRAIN
ANALYZE: FACTS, INFORMATION, EVIDENCE, PRECEDENT
Our analytical mind can figure it out when the hard data is known.

THE TRAP
WORRY: ANXIETY, FRUSTRATION, FEAR, STORIES, JUDGMENT
Our analytical mind cannot figure it out when the data is not available. We become anxious, distracted, and have a lack of focus. Our rational mind looks for evidence to support the worry.

RIGHT BRAIN
WONDER: REFLECT, IMAGINE, CREATE, ASK POSSIBILITY
Our intuitive mind has answers and information when the hard data is not available. This is a very creative part of us that generates new thinking.

As a caregiver you might feel that others expect you to have answers. You want to appear competent to your loved one and to the healthcare community. But you may be a far more effective caregiver if you become a good questioner.

Frame your caregiving as an opportunity for learning, and it will unfold more easily. Living as a learner is not only more peaceful, it is enlivening. Questions free you from the limitations of preconceived knowing, enabling you to embark on new waters.

Take a moment to reflect on and write about answers—those you feel others expect of you and those you expect of yourself. Begin to wonder about each one and you'll feel the uplift of shifting to your intuitive learning mind.

JOURNALING PROMPTS ON LEARNING

Turn to your caregiving journal and respond to the following:

1. Think about caregiving problems you feel required to solve. List them here. For each, what are the answers others expect of you? What signs of competence do you expect of yourself?

2. Try for a moment to suspend others' expectations of you and caregiving, and also your own expectations. What do you notice? Do new perspectives suggest themselves? What would be possible for you or others without those expectations?

3. Write down five things you are worried about, are afraid of, or things that just seem wrong. For each, generate a statement of wonder. If you are worried about your loved one's death, wonder what might death mean to others. Are you anxious about meeting a certain doctor? Begin to wonder what questions you could ask that would reveal his/her philosophy of healing. If another's behaviors seem wrong for the circumstances, what could the benefits of them be? Wonder if the behaviors even matter.

4. Write down a few times when intuitive, creative, right brain thinking has been most useful to you. Exactly how was it useful? What was possible that would not have been possible using left brain thinking?

In Part I we've covered the three core Mindful Caregiving principles:

- Be present;
- Shift your communications; and
- Welcome change.

We've looked at being present to your choices, your thoughts, and to self-awareness. We've talked about the power of shifting the way you think, speak and listen. And we've looked at the freedom to move that can be achieved by posing questions, moving from resisting to allowing, and opening yourself to right-brain learning.

In Part II we'll start to apply all of these principles to the three key areas of your caregiving experience: your emotions; your well-being; and your personal effectiveness.

Resources for Embracing Change

Books

When Everything Changes, Change Everything: In a Time of Turmoil, a Pathway to Peace by Neale Donald Walsch

Repacking Your Bags: Lighten Your Load for the Rest of Your Life by Richard J. Leider, David A. Shapiro

When Life Changes or You Wish It Would: A Guide to Finding Your Next Step Despite Fear, Obstacles, or Confusion, by Carol Adrienne

This Book Will Change Your Life, by Benrik

Transitions: Making Sense of Life's Changes, by William Bridges

Websites

Coping with Change and Loss www.extension.umn.edu

John Muir Health www.johnmuirhealth.com

Livestrong www.livestrong.com

Embracing change Blog www.embracingchangeaward.blogspot.com

Part Two

Applying The Principles
to Caregiving

Your Emotional Terrain

By staying present, speaking effectively, and practicing acceptance, you will gain greater freedom of movement in relation to your feelings. You will develop facility in managing your emotions. You will loosen the restrictive ties of hidden expectations. And you will plug the vitality drain of your resistance.

Your Personal Well-being

Here, as you stay present, speak effectively, and practice acceptance, you will learn secrets for keeping your inner light lit. You will build your network of support. And you will finally move with some grace through the rough caregiving waters to the open waters of the rest of your life.

Your Effectiveness

Staying present, speaking effectively, and practicing acceptance, will establish your effectiveness during caregiving and beyond. You will design new commitments to fuel your progress. You will utilize aspects of your family history. And you will learn to use your personality traits to fulfill your goals.

CHAPTER FOUR

APPLYING THE PRINCIPLES
TO YOUR EMOTIONS

And the day came when the risk it took
to remain tight inside the bud was more painful
than the risk it took to blossom.
—Anais Nin

In the usual course of caregiving events things can be chugging along nicely, feeling like a known quantity, and then life hits you broadside. It could be a sudden health issue, a change in your loved one's personality, or a failure of one of your carefully constructed supports. These out-of-nowhere snags are not system failures—they are simply part of the caregiving package. Success now and along the way will depend on where you focus your awareness. To get your bearings when trouble hits, first take a deep breath. Then look at the breadth of your life. You are part of a much bigger picture than it sometimes feels.

As this chapter unfolds, you will learn creative techniques for tuning your resilience as you navigate. You will begin to be more comfortable with risk during the ebb and flow of caregiving. You will learn how to adjust your degree of sensitivity. You will see that, despite fear, you can stay present while using anger to your benefit, as well as other lessons from the whole of your life.

If we let things terrify us,
life will not be worth living.
—Seneca, Epistles

Alive In Fear

If you want to shift the way you relate to fear, know your fear. Is it fear of risk? Fear of change? Fear of anger or of loss? Aspects of upbringing can contribute to a fearful response to life. Some of us simply have a fearful nature. You probably want your loved one to think the best of you. Perhaps you want him/her to see the highly functioning adult that you've become. Are you unnerved by the switch of roles that happens in caregiving? Now you are the responsible one. Has your loved one always been there for you but is weakening? Now you must be the strong one. How will he/she age? How will you know how to respond?

While these thoughts are normal they are also emotionally laden and fear-driven, lacking obvious answers. Fear takes you out of the moment into an imagined future that doesn't serve you. There are more useful places to focus. Fear, however, can also serve as a reminder to focus on the moment and just do the best that you can. That really is all that you can do. Some days you will fall short of your ideal. The world does not end. Once fear has captured your attention, you can reclaim your authority over your emotions by managing your thoughts.

Let us consider a worst-case scenario, one of those that appears to be life-threatening, as did Mom's broken ankle five days before her planned move into her apartment. It was Christmas night. I had driven her back to her retirement community. Walking slowly up the path, she shooed me away, telling me to go home. Shortly after I arrived home, a nurse phoned. Mom had fallen.

The moment that her ankle bone snapped we were shot into an alternate universe. As can happen with elders on pain meds, she was crazed with hallucinations. She believed people were coming to kill her, and that I was *in cahoots* with them. As I sat bound to her bedside as her scapegoat, I recalled a funeral at which a close friend of the deceased stood and said, "The audience of my life has fallen." Perhaps my purpose was simply to bear witness. I wondered if she might contract pneumonia and die right then. I had no way of knowing and no say in it. Resisting like mad, I sat for three days, present to my not-knowing, and allowing it to be. As I thought about my resistance and the unknowns, I thought of something that I *did* know, something I had learned from a relevant experience.

I had once taken an advanced driver training course taught on the runway of the local airport. As I swerved between rubber cones at 60-mph, I learned to disassociate the smell of burning rubber and the shriek of tires from *I'm going to die*. At Mom's bedside and throughout our decade together, I reminded myself that the unexpected isn't necessarily life threatening.

In turmoiled moments when there is little time for contemplation, three little questions can help to clarify your appropriate next step. Is this a true crisis, a life or death issue? If not, what is Really happening? (Is this urgent or merely a misperception?) And, what is my appropriate role in this and who can help?

A few moments of reflection can save time and stress. Conserving your energy needs to be a primary goal, right up there with supporting your loved one. Unnecessary anticipation of crises can cause an over-reaction to unexpected events. Someone else could be the more appropriate one to handle a situation. And even if it is yours to resolve, it is never wrong to ask who could shoulder some of the burden.

But what about when there is no imminent danger? What about the pervasive fear that can color the fabric of caregiving? Step one is to identify your fear. Remember, what you resist persists. Naming your fear, examining it, and then letting it be frees it to evolve. You then become stronger. There's fragility in needing to know or understand. Accept that the future holds unknowns, and you will be freer to experience the present. You will begin to trust your instincts, your ability to do the right thing.

None of us gracefully handles every moment. Gradually we learn to roll with it, fears and all. We resist. We notice. We step back with humor and self-compassion and we roll with it. Aikido is a martial art called "The Way of harmonious spirit." This self-defense discipline teaches us that when a force is moving toward us, if we counter that force head-on, we could get hurt. But if we begin to move in the same direction as the force, we instantly gain some control and can redirect the power of that force. Like caregiving Aikido masters, you can step aside and then move *with* the force of the moment. Moving with the prevailing wind you maintain control, allowing fear to be. Then you can speak in a way that keeps you in the present moment, where you can generate acceptance, gratitude, or any number of life-supporting emotions.

Acquaint yourself with your fear by answering the following questions in your journal.

Journaling Prompts on Fear

Turn to your caregiving journal and respond to the following:

1. What is your style of engaging with crises? Do you resist them when they crop up? Do you complain about them? Do you leap to action? Stop and think? Talk the situation over with a trusted person? Go into meltdown? Write down some of the phrases you say to yourself when a crisis hits, and your automatic response.

2. Make a list of the aspects of your caregiving that are known. Then list the unknowns that preoccupy your mind.

3. Which of the unknowns would you be willing to accept? Which can you imagine allowing to simply be there as you go about your day? Which ones do you believe will be resolved at some point, though you don't know exactly how?

4. What is the one aspect of caregiving that has been most bothering you? Write it down. Invent on the page various ways you might think about it. Could it be a gift? A learning? Just a normal part of caregiving? Is there a way of responding to it that would be unusual for you, one that would better serve you and others? Shift the way you hold it and respond to it, and you shift your experience of it.

(Harmony) is when...
"Yes" is tempered by a gentle "No,"
and "No" is expanded with measured compassion.
—Mrs. Chana Rachel Schusterman

MOVING BOUNDARIES

Regardless of our history or religious roots, society presents us with the moral imperative to honor our loved ones. When honoring means caregiving, a flurry of emotions arise, especially when relations have been less than ideal.

Excessive resistance to the thought of caregiving can come, at the extremes, from caring too much or from feeling too little. Few of us have struck the perfect balance between empathy and self-preservation. It is possible to be so entangled in love for a person that the thought of watching her/his decline feels impossible. Or if your loved one historically has been abusive either emotionally or physically, you likely feel an aversion to getting that close. Too much caring can swamp you, making you ineffective. Too little feeling will limit your caregiving to just basic maintenance. You could lose a precious opportunity, if not for relatedness, then for personal completion.

If either case feels familiar to you, yet you have decided to take on caregiving, you can find a healthy and effective middle ground between caring and emotional safety. Your boundaries define that middle ground by determining your emotional accessibility. They are the lines that limit how much or how little of yourself you will give. They are the point where you stop.

For instance, if you feel empathetic to your loved one to the point of entanglement, your vulnerability will make caregiving a struggle. If this sounds familiar to you, do you experience entanglement in other relationships? Learning how to extricate yourself, to reclaim an empowered sense of autonomy, will make you more effective and make all of life easier. A good therapist can facilitate this repositioning of boundaries. The normal changing of roles during caregiving can also rebalance your relationship. If your loved one becomes somewhat childlike, your adult self will naturally take its place in the relationship. Adjusting to this shift takes time. You can find yourself both grieving and celebrating the change. Be patient with yourself.

On the other extreme, if your loved one was unreliable or brutal when you were a child, and you responded by shutting down your emotions, your challenge will be different. If being with your loved one feels emotionally unsafe, consider contributing minimally or long distance. But if, as an adult, you have managed to gain some emotional distance on your shared history, this could be an opportunity for you and your loved one. You may never be best friends, but you might achieve greater peace. Is it worth it to you to try? If it seems right and wise to attempt to resolve your feelings, compassion could be the key to making the shift. You will need to stretch yourself, to work up some acceptance of who your loved one is, shortcomings and all. This doesn't mean that what they have done was right—only that they are who they are. The seeds of who (s)he is may have been planted before you were born. Understanding and acceptance breed compassion. Compassion will allow you your fullest possible expression of caregiving and self-expression in all of your relationships. Making such a shift is challenging, but can be facilitated with the help of a therapist.

As a child I stayed safe by emotionally detaching, but there was a price. I had trouble connecting fully with anyone, including myself. By mid-life I had healthier relationships. I could trust others and share myself. Then came the acid test—risking intimacy with Mom. In order to be truly of service to Mom, I knew I would have to unzip my heart and work up some compassion. To cultivate compassion, I imagined myself being her. I reflected in my diary on the inner experience of aging:

> *Some people shrink inside when they get old. Lose your senses and the world loses its vastness. Worlds contract as you focus inward. You breathe more slowly, get used to less, consume less. Eyes see in generalities, lacking the specifics of detail or distance. Ears hear noise with meaning muffled beneath cotton batting. Sometimes it's worth digging. Sometimes not. How much does not exist now that ears don't work well? Now that the inner ear no longer resonates with the hum of life setting the ear drum drumming? Oh God, the sounds, the heartbeat of life! I don't want to be one of the shrinking ones.*

To keep caring *for* Mom, I chose to care *about* her. Caring gave me the resilience to persist. Compassion made things tolerable, even forgivable. With compassion you become more present and resilient in all of your relationships.

Caregiving could redeem your past and emancipate your future. Whether you are cleaning up the residue of a painful past or extricating yourself from loving bondage, caregiving done well enables future freedom of spirit.

Now look at your boundaries in relations to your loved one and, using these questions, consider how you could move them. Write your thoughts in your journal.

JOURNALING PROMPTS ON BOUNDARIES

Turn to your caregiving journal and respond to the following:

1. Do you feel an aversion to the intimacy that caregiving will require? Write a description of your feelings. Name them. Be as specific as you can.

2. Does your attachment to your loved one feel so strong as to make you less effective? Write down some steps you could take to practice pulling back. Handling the more challenging moments in caregiving will require you to exert strength and authority. When might you practice saying No? Could you start each day thinking first about what you will do for yourself? If you are bound by a routine of visiting your loved one, when could you break that routine to do something special for yourself? How are you willing to carve out your own personal space?

3. Has your history with your loved one had challenging aspects, leaving you feeling emotionally distant? What in your loved one's history made them who they are? Note her/his personality traits that are stumbling blocks. What is the cost of each to relationships? In what ways is (s)he simply doing the best that (s)he can? What positive traits has your loved one passed on to you?

4. Regardless of your history, what are the ways you will maintain boundaries that feel comfortable to you? Make a list. This is a commitment to yourself. List changes in you, your thinking, or your routines that will empower you while letting your loved one manage their own aging process as much as possible.

Anger is a signal,
and one worth listening to.
—Harriet Lerner, The Dance of Anger

LEARNING FROM ANGER

As a culture we are confused about anger. Is anger a good thing to let out? Or is it an inappropriate self-indulgence? How can we manage it well if we're not sure how to think about it? Might it even be useful to us during caregiving? A providential moment of anger, when well managed, can return forward movement to life. It can put you back in the driver's seat. If wielded wisely, it can be a catalyst for positive change.

In his book *Power vs. Force: The Hidden Determinants of Human Behavior*, David R. Hawkins ranks emotions by their energy level. Your personal energy level is determined by your prevailing emotional state. The higher your energy level, the more positively alive you are. According to Hawkins, anger is a higher-energy emotion than fear, apathy or grief. Anger's energy can pull you up from such lower-level states and get you moving forward again. A providential moment of anger, when well managed, can put you back in the driver's seat.

Steven Covey, corporate change guru and author of *The 7 Habits of Highly Effective People*, says power is, "the faculty or capacity to act, the strength and potency to accomplish something." One caregiving goal can be to optimize your power. Anger can kick-start your power if you learn how to use it well. Learning how to use your anger can be an act of self-preservation. Anger is normal. Not only that, within limits it can be healthy and useful. We're not talking about pathological anger that is unleashed as a weapon to damage or control others. Rather this is the domesticated variety that can be a useful signpost to important lessons.

The following are some advantages of anger:

- Anger lets you know what you are ignoring. It shows you when you are neglecting your own needs. If you are over-tired, haven't taken time for yourself, haven't been exercising or eating properly, you might over-react to things you would normally handle well. Instead of making light of anger as an over-reaction, pay close attention. In caregiving your peace of mind is a survival goal. Think about what you could add to your life to improve your stamina and boost your well-being. Then change your lifestyle.

- Anger can also raise its head when you are resisting an aspect of life that you would be better off accepting. Caregiving gets smoother when you look at what you're resisting, and find ways to accept what you cannot change. Rather than minimizing your reaction, look at it closely. Understand it. Be understanding of yourself. Over time your resistance (and anger) will shift and recede. You will grow as you increase your capacity to embrace all of life.

- If you have unrealistic expectations of yourself, others, the medical community, or caregiving, you have set yourself up for anger. Life simply can't measure up, so try lowering or changing your expectations. In chapter six, we'll be discussing when it is important to do battle, but if an issue isn't critical, couldn't you let it slide? Think of yourself as partnering with the medical community, with aides, and with siblings. An unnecessarily combative stance in relations to any aspect of your life can breed bitterness and anger. Focus on simply doing your part. That is always the only thing you can do.

- Finally, anger can show you when you need to speak up about something. The feelings from which constructive anger arises are often valid and understandable. In a sermon on anger and forgiveness, Unitarian Universalist Reverend Kendra Ford says "I'm advocating actually being angry, getting angry, staying angry for a while... Anger is the response when someone forgets the wholeness and self-determination of your being or other people's... It's the emphatic and self-possessed no! And it has life only in the present." Rather than tamping down feelings, explore them. Look at them. Write about them. Look for ways of sharing your feelings authentically in a way that is non-combative.

We'll be talking more about how to communicate effectively. For now, look for ways to learn from your anger, to use it to your advantage. Begin your exploration by writing in response to the following questions.

JOURNALING PROMPTS ON ANGER

Turn to your caregiving journal and respond to the following:

1. On a scale from one to ten, with one being not at all, and ten being immobilized, to what degree do you feel victim to others or your circumstances? Who are the people? What are the circumstances? What do your feelings about each of them have in common? Do you see ways in which you may have been relinquishing your power?

2. What are your strategies for managing anger? If you tend to stuff down your anger, what are other ways you could address it? If you need to speak up to someone about something, write down what you need to say in its simplest expression. "I need you to back off." "You're expecting too much of me." "You were rude to me and I would like an apology." Determining what is yours to handle and what belongs to someone else can be tricky. In which cases could you simply let it go?

3. Or are you more familiar with depression than with anger? Depression can conceal anger just beneath the surface. If this could be you, can you visualize yourself allowing a flicker of anger to rise in you, to live in you long enough to take a good look at it? Explore it. Write down whatever comes up for you.

4. List a few recent times when you felt something like anger. Next to each note the apparent cause. Then note any underlying causes, going deeper and deeper until you believe you have the root cause for each. Do the root causes point the way to new remedial action? Is there some false expectation that you can address? Or some aspect of yourself, someone else, or caregiving that you would do well to accept?

When you are walking on thin ice,
you might as well dance.
—Anon

EMBRACING RISK

Saying Yes to caregiving feels risky. So what do we do with that? At first, though you do not yet have an understanding of the risks, you do have your inner assets operating in your favor. You have your past experiences on which to draw, and the strategies and tactics you have developed for survival. Some serve you well, and some don't. Let's begin by teasing apart some of the aspects of risk-taking so that you can know it better.

A good first step in exploring the meaning of risk-taking is to notice the times in your life when you took big risks and they paid off. Part of you was probably looking for any way to take the safe route, the path of lesser change. But what were your motivators for taking risk? What was big and important enough to you? This is what came up first for me when I first thought about it.

Looking back at my life, I saw that my most treasured experiences had required risk. In the first years of my caregiving I saw that my marriage, a then 25-year life experience, had at numerous times required risking change in order to thrive. This opportunity to be with Mom during her final years had that same quality of now-or-never that I recognized from the major choice points in my marriage. As with those marital turning points, something big was at stake. Both challenges required deciding the kind of person I was willing to be and the kind of life for which I was willing to stick out my neck.

Next, begin to look at your motivations for taking on caregiving. Yours may be quite different from mine, but you will see the kind of inquiry that I am suggesting. Asking Mom to live near me was a terrifying step into the unknown. In a poem I described my childhood as *Barbed wire years until one day, a-tiptoe through the compound, and I'd cut and run before she caught my scent.* A number of things drove me to take the leap, but at its root the choice came out of an irrational love for my mother, and a few fundamental commitments. First, I felt the urge to do the right and honorable thing. Second, I knew it would be an education in life, and I've had a long-standing commitment to learning. And then there was my commitment to myself to live life fully.

Finally, consider all of the positive factors that you have operating in your favor. Look at the ways in which caregiving is an opportunity for you, your loved one, and your family. When I took on caregiving, I was 45. I was a life-long learner. I was no longer the child that my mother remembered. I knew that, somehow, I could do it. This time I was being offered a chance to be part of the cycle of life, to hold hands with my mother as she faced her dying. I said to myself, *Take this chance and you'll walk away a more whole person. You won't regret it. The chance won't come again.*

Practical considerations occupy the forefront at first, but at its root, entering into caregiving is a choice made in your gut. Though we may be used to making the bigger life decisions with a logical, practical mindset, in caregiving a surprising number of the most important decisions will be (and I say should be) informed by intuition, gut, a right-brain sense of what is right.

As I moved through caregiving, my intuition became my strongest ally. Understanding my relationship with risk freed up my intuition to operate in my favor. This duality I had identified in myself, these seemingly opposed priorities of safety and risk, I now saw as a source of great strength. I knew I could stretch myself, take sensible risks, and that my experience would be richer as a result. Safety and risk were not at odds. My belief about a full life requiring change and risk kept me moving forward through caregiving.

In an article in the Jerusalem Post, 11/4/09, titled *In My Own Write: Embracing Risk,* Judy Montagu tells of a young woman who bicycled down the highest motorable road in the world: the 18,380 foot Khardung La pass in India. The woman said, "I didn't want to do the bike ride at first, but then I decided that I would take it slowly and see how it went... At the end, I had done it in spite of being scared. It gave me a good feeling about myself - that I was stronger than I had thought. I felt more confident about what I could do." She had taken a risk, and it had helped her grow. Montagu continues, "Is risk better avoided? I'm convinced there are areas where it needs to be actively embraced."

What you value and believe, the things you say are true about life, give you reality as you know it. They both limit and expand your experience. How have you felt about risk? There are numerous aspects of life and caregiving that can feel risky. Only you know what those are for you. The better you understand what you classify as risk, the more quickly you will feel greater safety. True safety is grounded in a strong belief in your own ability to embrace risk and thrive.

Now journal a bit to gain clarity about risk's role in your caregiving.

JOURNALING PROMPTS ON RISK

Turn to your caregiving journal and respond to the following:

1. What values and beliefs have determined the path of your life? Make a list of the ones that informed your major choices at key turning points in your life. They might include loyalty, gratitude, love, freedom, connection, procreation, self-expression, adventure, and many more. How were these life choices influenced by issues of safety and risk?

2. How have you related to risk and safety in the past? Jot down a few of the biggest risks you have taken. These could be risks in which you knew the possible outcomes, or risks for which you had no idea of the outcomes.

3. Which risks were thrust upon you and which were freely chosen? How did you feel about each? Which risks have expanded or limited your life and in what ways? Write any thoughts about them here. Circle the ones that you would risk again.

4. What risks face you in caregiving? What do you risk losing? What do you risk gaining? List them here. In the face of those, what calls you to keep moving forward? For the sake of what goal or benefit are you willing to welcome these unknowns?

*Learning from experience is
a faculty almost never practiced.*
—Barbara Tuchman

Capitalizing on Life Lessons

Your regular life doesn't go on hold just because you have taken on the role of caregiver. Other major challenges offer valuable growth that translates directly into a more competent, confident caregiving experience. Behaviors during other crises can closely parallel the way you choose to act as a caregiver. Think of these other life challenges as training in how you could think about caregiving.

The way that I responded to my cancer had direct implications for the ways that I could respond to caregiving. For me, life all of a sudden got very much more precious. I noticed the way I was thinking and the actions that I took. All of these approaches I then brought to bear on my approach to caregiving.

- I was philosophical: What's to be angry about? It was just my turn. I was practical: What a waste of time to wallow in undirected anger. There are important things to be doing.

- I accepted the reality of the experience and got on with the job at hand, stopping and noticing my life

- I was grateful for friends and loved ones, while cleaning out life's deadwood of shallow relationships and meaningless obligations.

- I made room for what was vital and sustaining.

- I became a warrior, primed to battle whatever was necessary in order to move forward.

- I was a learner, learning everything that I could about alternative medicine, and later, geriatric medicine.

- I didn't compromise—I designed support systems for myself, and later, for my mother.

- I allowed for changing needs. With cancer, as with caregiving,

relationships shifted. The definition of support changed as my
needs changed, and it was up to me to communicate my needs. In
caregiving I not only had to tend to my own needs, I had to identify
Mom's shifting needs.

- I let love heal. Recognizing during cancer how valued and loved I
was by friends and family became a significant piece of my healing.
Valuing and loving myself while learning to love my mother made
caregiving a process of even deeper healing.

- I did what I could and let that be enough. In both cancer and
caregiving I was determined that, in the end, I would be able to say
I had done all that I could. That was another one of my caregiving
mantras.

- I focused on my blessings. In cancer, as in caregiving, I saw many
ways in which the siege had been a mind, heart, and life expanding
experience. I had identified my true friends. My marriage was
stronger and more flexible. I could communicate my needs. Asking
for help strengthened me, making me less rigid and brittle. My
cancer survivor friends said much the same things—cancer brought
with it invaluable blessings. So does caregiving.

When thinking about caregiving, notice if you begin to compartmentalize life,
separating the caregiving you from the everyday you. Compartmentalizing your life
may give you the illusion of greater control, but such a split not only fractures life, it
prevents benefiting from the crossover learnings that life is offering.

What lessons has life taught you about love, forgiveness, resilience, or any of
the many aptitudes that let us live well? The more holistic your thinking about life's
lessons, the more whole you will be as a caregiver, lover, nurturer, and friend.

Now, take a step back to take a look at your life lessons by answering the
following questions.

JOURNALING PROMPTS ON LIFE LESSONS

Turn to your caregiving journal and respond to the following:

1. List down the left of the page any challenges or crises that you either have currently in your life, or have had in the past.

2. Next to each, list your thoughts or reactions to what happened. What did you learn from each about yourself, life, or someone else?

3. Then list words that describe the way you coped in response to each. Were you forthright, a problem-solver, or did you seek spiritual solitude? What part of your personality was called out?

4. Of these qualities that you saw in yourself, which could you use to strengthen your caregiving experience? What new ways of responding to life could you learn that would serve you and your loved one?

When you are sorrowful look again in your heart,
and you shall see that in truth you are weeping
for that which has been your delight.
—Kahlil Gibran

Curtailing Pregrieving

We humans have a habit of practicing life ahead of time, running our minds and hearts down the track of anticipated events, trying to increase our ability to cope with what is to come. It's as though we are basketball players going through our mental moves to increase our effectiveness for an upcoming game. Yet when thinking of an impending loss, we are more likely to anticipate the difficulties than we are to envision ourselves successfully coping. If what we think determines what we get, which would you rather choose to manifest? Success or trouble?

Since caregiving is concentrated living, it brings a denser experience of emotions and challenges. The highs and lows feel more extreme than in ordinary life. At times you could find yourself spending undue energy in anticipation of your grief, as I did. In my diary, I wrote:

Mom, John and I greeted this new century by writing our regrets and dreams on little pieces of paper. Our regrets went into the fireplace. Our dreams we tied to the strings of helium balloons, letting them fly straight up into the stars. The universe has them now. Feels like a beginning. But how do you finish a life? We keep plugging as though nothing is out of the ordinary. Mom and I both know that she is slipping. I'm afraid of her losing her mind slowly, drop by drop, as I watch her drift, then come back to me.

I have become increasingly convinced that excessive pregrieving does us no good at all. How often have your major life events turned out to be just as you had imagined? If you are married, has it turned out to be what you expected? If you have children, has parenthood unfolded as anticipated? In my experience major life events are sometimes better, sometimes worse. Those that are billed as happy can turn out to be harder than we had imagined. Those that we expected to be tragic can carry with them great joy. Even the death of your loved one will be different from your imaginings.

In an article entitled, *Pre-grief: Is something gained in letting go before something is lost?* (Mindreadersdictionary.com) professor and writer Jeremy Sherman explores various ways to think about pregrief. "The Tao says, 'Success is as dangerous as failure; hope is as hollow as fear.' Every increase in happiness means that much more to grieve in the end. Adore your new pet cat? You'll lose it. Fall madly in love? You'll lose it. All ups have downs, so maybe we should try to even it out by starting to grieve the loss of the cat the day we get it."

The Hospice organization sheds further light on our misconceptions about anticipatory grief. "Originally there was this notion when somebody had a terminal or even questionable prognosis, the family might start grieving their loss in anticipation of death," says Kenneth Doka, PhD, a professor of gerontology at the College of New Rochelle and senior consultant to the Hospice Foundation of America. "It led to this notion that you could almost finish your grieving prior to death." The theory goes that a mourner has only so many tears to spend; the more that are shed beforehand, the fewer there will be after. "Unhelpful," says Doka.

If what you resist persists, it follows that what you focus on manifests. Expecting pain makes its manifestation more likely. By imagining pain you may be limiting the range of emotions available to you when the feared events do transpire. Your state of mind will benefit from letting go of the need to know how the future will feel.

Excessive pregrieving can also take a toll on your physical health. Weighing your spirit down with dark imaginings of what is to come can only take you away from your vitality in the moment. A weighted spirit breeds a weakened immune system. Your physical, spiritual and emotional health call on you to pay attention to the present moment. It is all that you have. Live your present as fully as possible. When your mind goes into its "bad neighborhood," stop and recognize that your thoughts are fabrications.

Most of us have activities that center us in the present moment. Some meditate, some do physical labor, some create artwork, bake, or work on the car. Do what you can to pull yourself back. Do the activities that drop you into the present.

Take a moment now to reflect on pregrieving, writing down whatever comes up for you.

JOURNALING PROMPTS ON PREGRIEVING

Turn to your caregiving journal and respond to the following:

1. When in the past have you indulged in pregrieving? What was the impact on your energy level? On your peace of mind? On your effectiveness?

2. Are there specific times of day, people, or circumstances that bounce you into pregrieving? List them here. How could you manage each situation differently? Circle the places or people you would do well to avoid.

3. Conversely, what are the people, places, or activities that could pull you back into the present, perhaps by providing a diversion? Which ones put you back on the right track? Circle the ones that you are willing to build into your life.

4. Write down an exhaustive list of statements of gratitude that could replace future thoughts of pregrieving.

Finish each day and be done with it. You have done what you could.
Tomorrow is a new day; begin it well and serenely and with
too high a spirit to be encumbered with your old nonsense.
—Ralph Waldo Emerson

WEATHERING CALM & STORMY WATERS

Caregiving is no steady state, as it brings both periods of turmoil and periods of unexpected calm. If your loved one's medical team is expanding you can suddenly have doctors, nurses, and aides with whom to establish workable relations. A changing list of treatments and prescriptions requires research. Monitoring finances adds a new level of complexity. There is simply more to manage than there was before.

At some point medical incidents become more frequent When the first major crisis hits, the stakes suddenly feel higher, as I found out. I wrote in my diary:

My moods have been swinging, ape-like. Last Sunday I was crazed, racing around the kitchen. Dropping things. Careening from counter to fridge, cupboard to chopping block, a dangerous chef. Yet when I step back to look, I see I've been operating on good instincts with some serendipity. I've never played this part before and yet I'm responding appropriately. When things go wildly out of balance, I right myself. At times I feel guilty that I haven't done enough or that I've trusted professionals too much. Then I remind myself to be compassionate. I am doing the best that I can. It is all I can do.

The summer of our seventh year began with a ride to the hospital. The red lights flashed spookily ahead of me. I thought, *It's my mom in there! Dear God, Thy will be done. If this is the end, let it happen as easily as possible.* Then again, I knew this could well be merely the first of many such moments. I'd better get used to it—it's all training in living with the unknown. I thought back to what I had learned.

- If I don't know exactly what is true then there is now nothing to mourn.
- Since my experience is determined by what I focus on and my emotions are determined by the stories I choose to tell myself, then I had better take charge of my imagination and make up something good for heaven's sake!

When you observe emotions from a slight distance, accepting the fact of them, you are less at sway to the unexpected. You carry with you many learnings. Use your intuition. By now you have some understanding of your role. Your support team is there for you—tell them when your needs change. If you need more support, expand your team by adding a counselor or a workshop. You are more resilient than before. You have options.

By contrast, the times of no real movement can be a surprising challenge. Suddenly there is neither progress to celebrate nor problems to tackle. No change to navigate. No new knowledge to acquire. The days have a surreal quality, like sitting becalmed in a vast ocean, or wandering through mist. How long can life go on like this? You are most present to the unknowns of it all. What will the next phase bring? What should I do to keep going one day after the next?

As always, there is one thing over which you do have control—your attitude. With the right state of mind you can use this time. These are the times for faith, for focusing on being rather than doing. At some point in the future, life will again move forward. For now, acknowledge what is. Do what you can, then focus on inner things.

As the March winds blew around the old house, Mom began to imagine things in the middle of the night. As James Thurber wrote of his grandmother, "She lived... in the horrible suspicion that electricity was dripping invisibly all over the house." The days seemed to go on and on, some days nice, other days freaky, but there was nothing in particular we could do about it. One day her fears would keep her in her chair rather than exercising. The next, her fear of immobility had her rising to the occasion of life. She'd perk up and want to go for a walk. One day she burst out with, "I want to be forward-looking!" Golly! Good for her! I swung between rejoicing in these happier moments, and fearing her end. As she lost her grip on life I would lose my hold on her. I knew that doing a little pregrieving was appropriate, but I didn't want to lose myself in wallowing. I needed to learn to hold life more lightly, so I adopted a new attitude to keep me going. I thought of the lucid, fun, sharing times as what was normal, and the other times as just freak trips away until she came back to me. And I lightened up. I did things that uplifted me. When I found myself grieving, I thought of our good times, so as to fully honor the path we had taken together. Eventually, Mom's fears had her admit that it was time to move to an assisted living home.

You are not the cause, and you are not the solution. You are part of a complex story that is playing out. You need only do your part. Take note of the gifts that life presents each day; the cycles of nature, sweet strains of a favorite piece of music, the things that sustain you. You are only one small part of this great rhythm of life.

The following questions will reveal the ebb and flow of your caregiving.

JOURNALING PROMPTS ON CALM & STORMY TIMES

Turn to your caregiving journal and respond to the following:

1. When are your calm and your stormy times? What are the life circumstances of each? How do your emotions shift from day to day, or week to week? When do you resist? When do you release control? Document your emotional ebb and flow.

2. In the calm and stormy times, what are the limited sets of things that you can do, as distinct from what you wish you could do? How might you take care of yourself so as to lighten the experience for everyone?

3. Of what are you afraid in the stormy times? Of what are you afraid in the calm times? Can you accept that what happens isn't up to you, that it isn't all on your shoulders?

4. What lightens your heart? What aspects of your life do you most cherish? Parts of your history with your loved one? Write about them.

In this chapter we have talked about a variety of ways to apply your three tools of being present, shifting your thinking, and embracing change in the realm of your emotions. We saw how to stay in motion through fear, and the ups and downs of caregiving. We looked at the value of adjusting emotional boundaries, as well as learning from anger, and from the lessons in other parts of your life. And we questioned the value of extensive pregrieving.

In the next chapter we will apply the three tools to the area of your well-being. We will see how you can balance your relationships and your life. We'll look at how to set your caregiving goals, recharge your spirit, and intentionally choose happiness.

RESOURCES

Books

Boundaries: When to Say Yes, How to Say No to Take Control of Your Life, by Henry Cloud

When I Say No, I Feel Guilty, by Manuel J. Smith

Broken Open: How Difficult Times Can Help Us Grow, by Elizabeth Lesser

Resilience: Reflections on the Burdens and Gifts of Facing Life's Adversities, by Elizabeth Edwards

The Places That Scare You: A Guide to Fearlessness in Difficult Times, by Pema Chodron

When Things Fall Apart, by Pema Chodron

It's All in Your Head: Thinking Your Way to Happiness, by Stephen M. Pollan

Writing for Emotional Balance: A Guided Journal To Help You Manage Overwhelming Emotions, by Beth Jacobs

Power vs. Force: The Hidden Determinants of Human Behavior, David R. Hawkins

Magazines & Websites

Psychology Today www.psychologytoday.com

Scientific American Mind www.scientificamerican.com/sciammind

Aging with Grace www.agingwithgrace.net

Emotional Balance www.wholesomebalance.com

Chapter Five

Applying the Principles to Your Well-being

The time will come
when, with elation
you will greet yourself arriving
at your own door, in your own mirror
and each will smile at the other's welcome
— Derek Walcott
        from "Love After Love"

While well-being sounds as simple as feeling good, the path to consistently achieving it can seem elusive. Most of our lives are run by assumptions, habitual behaviors, and automatic thinking, "habits of being" that collude to trip us up in our search for inner peace. Changing these habits requires first being present to how you are feeling, and then identifying exactly what is tripping you up. In that moment of standing back and observing, you can see what isn't working and be free to choose another way.

In this chapter we will apply the three tools, Be Present, Shift Communications, and Embrace Change, to your well-being as you rebalance yourself and your life. Step by step we will identify what you need to introduce into your life in order to have a consistent sense of well-being. You will learn how to ask for help. You will find ways to build self-connection and recharge your spirit. You will see the importance of self-care, choosing happiness and using humor to achieve balance and emotional health throughout caregiving.

*Few things can make us feel crazier than expecting something
from someone who has nothing to give.*
—Melody Beattie

Asking for Help

Asking for help isn't easy. It's a primary skill for successful caregiving. What makes it so hard to do? Asking for help is counter-cultural. Many of us are weaned on the message that going it alone is a sign of strength. Raised to be proud of our fortitude, we stoically forge ahead. Welcome to The Lone Ranger Syndrome. It weakens the fabric of relationships at home and at work. And in caregiving, this handicap does immeasurable damage to a caregiver's well-being.

Our ecology alerts us to an awareness that we are each a part of a greater whole. As members of a family, a community, and a world, we are interconnected. That interconnection keeps the web of life resilient and thriving. If we, as caregivers, can be open and willing, our connection to others can be one of our greatest assets.

Begin asking for help, and you'll learn something startling. Requesting help can be empowering. How can this be? Shakti Gawain observes that "You create your opportunities by asking for them." When you ask for help, you gain access to a world of solutions you would never have accessed alone. By the options that you entertain, you are made resilient. By the wisdom that you find, you are made stronger. Others' respect for you deepens.

There are a few different kinds of requests for help. Asking help of professionals is, hopefully, straightforward. There are whole organizations whose purpose it is to support caregivers. Seeking support from family members can be trickier. Who will get on board and work with you? Who will jump ship to take care of themselves? Who will try to contribute in ways that won't feel like a contribution? The needs and limitations of others may seem like obstacles to getting what you need. You will need to make room for others to be who they are, as you simultaneously and clearly communicate your own needs.

About two years into caregiving I began to feel afraid. Up until then I had been a good soldier, not saying much about my feelings about caregiving. My lack of communication had left me feeling very alone. I called my two sisters and asked if they would be willing to phone me once a week to check in. The eldest, who lived across the country, said yes, she would. My other sister, who lived two hours away, told me point blank that she couldn't promise to connect regularly. No explanation.

At first, I wondered what family meant to her, what sisterhood meant. I was hurt, confused, and angry. After sitting with my dark thoughts for a few weeks, I knew I was wasting my precious energy. I stopped to look at my thinking. What stood out were the specific assumptions that had given rise to my resentments. I had to wrestle my illusions of sisterhood to the ground, in order to accept her unexplained determination to keep her distance. I didn't need to know her reasons. I was able to summon some compassion for her because I knew that all three of us had difficulty being with Mom. Years later I learned that during Mom's decline, my sister had been grappling with a consuming private personal issue.

Even if you have healthy relationships, you are likely to make assumptions about how people will respond, and you could be wrong or disappointed. Siblings and partners have their own histories and can be unpredictable. Beware of slipping into judgment fueled by false assumptions. If you find that someone isn't as available to you as you would like, he or she could simply be doing the best that they can. Once you let go of your expectations about the way you wish they were responding, you can see more clearly what is possible and what is not.

The experience of asking for help can be full of surprises. People you thought would be there for you may disappear, while others you thought were too distant may step forward. Even seemingly small acts of involvement can keep the doorway of relationship open. And friends can step quietly forward out of the shared moments of daily living to fill the spaces untaken by blood relations.

Step by step, you will optimize your community of support, rethink the meaning of support, and find workable ways to communicate your requests. Life probably won't show up exactly as expected, but the path you forge will be uniquely yours as you gain resilience.

After asking for help wherever possible, you can re-assess your situation. If you are still coming up short, contact your local social service agencies or Senior Center. There may be free service in your area. There certainly will be people trained in the field of caregiving who can advise you about your options.

If, as you anticipate asking for help, you feel that you would like a clearer sense of how to have a successful conversation, a good therapist, counselor or life coach may be of help. These professionals can teach you about the various types of conversations, types of listening, body language, interaction of personality types and more.

The following guidelines will help set you up for requesting help. And the following journal prompts will shed light on the ways that you think about asking for help.

How to Ask for Help
A Sibling Example

1. DEFINE YOUR GOAL - First, define your Terms for Help simply "I need help with X for Y number of hours each week." Or "I want to know who I can depend on for what."

2. DUMP YOUR EXPECTATIONS - Your expectations will undermine you every time. Let's say you need to ask help of your sister. Identify your expectations of her. Then decide that if she agrees to help, whatever she can do is a blessing.

3. BE CLEAR ABOUT THE OTHER PERSON - Her life may be more complicated than you know. She may be having her own difficulty accepting your elder's decline.

4. BE CREATIVE, NOT DESPERATE - Don't threaten your relationship by hanging everything on this one conversation. An all-or-nothing stance leaves you wide open for resentment, an unnecessary drain on your energy. There are usually a number of ways to solve a problem.

5. BE CLEAR - Be clear within yourself and explicit in your words to her about exactly what you are asking for. Do you want to vent, and just have her listen? Or do you want advice? Do you want to brainstorm solutions to a problem? Do you want her to participate in some way (that works for her) to help resolve a problem? Being clear within yourself and speaking clearly to her greatly increase the chances that you will get helpful results.

6. BE GRACIOUS - If you come around to point blank asking your sister to pitch in, and she says No, listen to what is behind the no. Then thank her for considering it.

7. MAKE ROOM FOR THE UN-IMAGINED - Finally, if she has declined your request, ask her if there *is* something she would be willing to do to support you.

A Program for Getting Help

Turn to your caregiving journal and respond to the following:

1. List all of your activities, responsibilities, and needs. Don't forget your emotional needs. Include both commitments to others, and to yourself. Place a star beside the ones for which you can imagine having a helper, cheerleader, mentor or other form of support.

2. Whom do you see as your supporters or advocates? Who is "in your court?" List them here. Who else might be willing to help even in small ways? Add their names to the list. Then place a name or two next to each of the items on your first list. One person may be a great listener while another may be an action person who could help with small errands. Be creative in how you define your needs, how you think of help, and in how you think about who might be there for you.

3. Get out your telephone book and make a list of the organizations that support caregivers. If you have internet access, run a Google search for "help for caregivers" or "caregiver support." Familiarize yourself with the services in your area. If any look like appropriate additions to your support team, add them to the list of your supporters.

4. Set yourself a number of people or organizations that you will speak to each day to establish your support team. Explain to each that in order to do the caregiving to which you are committed, you need to know who might be willing to be supportive, even in the smallest ways. Tell each that "No" is a fine answer. You just need to know. If someone you wanted on your team is clearly unwilling, journal a bit about the factors that may be affecting their willingness. What will it take to get past your disappointment and accept them as they are with their limitations?

Once in a while you have to
take a break and visit yourself.
—Audrey Giorgi

BUILDING SELF-CONNECTION

Whether you leap or tiptoe into caregiving, you may unwittingly ignore your own needs or tamp down your emotions. Some of your biggest resources and major stumbling blocks will come from within you. In order to be effective as a caregiver, you will need to tune in to your own feelings, your needs, and your personal truth. This is not just your loved one's journey—it is also yours. Staying connected to yourself will allow you to be present so as to do your best caregiving.

During caregiving many of us live reactively, at the beck and call of career and family. Well-being requires balance—a balance between taking care of others and taking care of ourselves. Mastering balance calls for awareness. While most of us are keenly aware of others' needs, we can easily overlook our own.

In a rare, solitary moment you may hear an inner voice whisper, *What about me?* Isn't that selfish? No. Attending to yourself may sound like an indulgence, but during caregiving it is a necessity. This runs counter to what we are taught and to the way most of us arrange our priorities. Caregiving is an honorable gift to be giving your loved one. To do it well you will need to focus on your own needs.

Each of us has strategies developed in childhood for staying safe. My protection of choice was emotional distance from my own needs. In caregiving, life was calling on me to reconnect with myself. I was under greater stress than I knew and, for my own health, needed an emotional tune-up. I sought guidance from a book called *The Artist's Way*, by Julia Cameron. This brilliant book of insights and exercises is designed to help artists become creatively unstuck, to reconnect with their creativity. I used it a bit differently, thinking of my life as my art. It worked. It reconnected and unstuck me. I learned the value of writing daily morning pages (three pages of unedited brain dump) and I learned that I felt most in touch with myself when I wrote.

Shortly after Mom's arrival in New Hampshire, she bought me my first laptop. Unwittingly she gave me the means to keep my sanity when dealing with her. Early on, I wrote in my diary of the freedom I found in writing:

*I save my document when secretly I hope it will save me. Like dowsing for water, I am pulled
into deep experience to find the words that flow freely, dowsing for poetry in the earth of me.*

Through writing I learned emotional resilience that would nourish me throughout my
journey and beyond. I also connected with a more intuitive understanding of my caregiving
role. What self-connecting activities work for you? A long walk? Listening to music? Or is
inactivity or silence your preference?

So much of caregiving is anything but silence. Speaking is one way we have an
effect on our world, and our first instinct is to be effective. By email, phone, cell phone, and
in person we ask, tell, inquire, cajole, and explain, as we try to manage life. When there's
nothing to manage, the urge is to turn off the brain with diversions. Television, reading, or
a few drinks can feel essential. But rush too quickly to tune out, and you will miss potentially
healing moments of self-connection. When life isn't presenting you with tasks, allow the
silence to nurture, heal, and guide you.

In caregiving, intuition can be a bellwether guiding us to our best course of action.
Intuition requires self-connection. In moments of self-connection, from the space that is
created, our instinct and intuition have room to arise and guide us. In her book, *Connections*,
Gabrielle Roth teases out some of the more subtle obstacles to this gift of instinct, or
intuition. "Basically, instinct bypasses the brain, grabs the body, and lets you know loud and
clear what to do or not do... The problem is that when we live in our heads we may not hear
or feel our instincts. Or if we do, we may resist following them because we are insulated in a
cocoon of identities, personas—images of ourselves as someone who acts in a certain way...
Obsessing over what image you project to other people is a symptom of self-importance and
cuts you off from your instinct. In this state of being you think you know all the answers; in
fact, you probably think you are the answer... We need to let go of fixed ideas, behaviors,
attachments... Unfettered, your true self flows to the surface and moves you toward your
purpose, your destiny here on this earth."

Perhaps you're thinking, *I don't have the time for such self-focus.* But before you rush
headlong into your day, ask yourself how much of what you do is truly necessary and how
much is out of ill-considered habit? How much of your identity is bound up in being the
competent caregiver? If you were to take self-connection seriously, might your intuition offer
you answers, actions, and ways of being that would make caregiving far easier?

Now make room in your schedule for self-connection with the following exercise,
Housecleaning for Self-connection. Then the journal prompts will show you the
commitments you could eliminate, and self-connection you might explore.

HOUSECLEANING FOR SELF-CONNECTION MATRIX

1. Turn to a new page in your journal. Turn it sideways. List down the left side all of your activities in a given week. Then make five or six columns to the right.

2. At the tops of the columns put headings representing what you need more of in your life, like energy or money. You're going to be rating your activities and commitments according to which satisfy these needs. For instance, the chart could show you which activities cost money or make money, which ones give or take away your energy or time. Think of the things that you want more of in your life and you'll know what to put at the tops of the columns. Add as many columns as you need to reflect what is important to you.

3. Save a column to note which activities are for yourself and which are for others.

4. Below your chart, write a bit about what motivates you to do each of your activities. This will show you the values that drive your commitments. You may discover which values fuel you in your life and which ones don't.

5. Put plus/minus signs, letters or symbols in each of the columns to indicate the activities that take from you, and those that give back. Adapt the system so that it works for you. If an activity gives you a lot of energy, put two or three plus signs. If one takes just a little time, show a small "t". If an activity is for others, but you get pleasure out of it too, put both an O for "Others" and an S for "Self." It will begin to look something like this:

Activity	Money	Energy	Time	Self/Other
Visit Mom	-	- -	TT	s/o
Church	-$	++	t	s
Kids	n/a	-	TTT	s/o
Lunch w/ friends	-$	+++	t	SS
Work	+$$	- -	TTT	s/O

(exercise, cont'd.)

6. Write down all of your insights as you look at your completed matrix. Is it severely out of balance in any aspect? Which activities would you be better off not doing?

7. On a new page, list the people in your life. Use this same system to rate them according to who gives or takes energy, who makes your life simpler or more complex, who supports you and who doesn't. Housecleaning comes in many forms.

JOURNALING PROMPTS ON SELF-CONNECTION

Turn to your caregiving journal and respond to the following:

1. Throughout your life, who have been your models for self-connection? Write their names here. Note how each of them modeled self-connection. What does self-connection mean to you?

2. Is there some aspect of yourself with which you have become disconnected? Some part of you not lately used that might serve you in the coming months or years? In the past have you written poetry or journaled? Gone for meditative walks? Had a spiritual practice? Played a musical instrument? Write down whatever comes to mind.

3. List the aspects of your life you are willing to eliminate to clear the way for greater freedom. These are the activities, commitments and people from which you are willing to back away, either temporarily or permanently.

4. Write up your Self-connection Master Plan. Include all the changes in your routines that will streamline your life, as well as dates for accomplishing each change. Include new ideas for things that will bring greater self-connection. Could you see more of creative friends? Could you find a spiritual center or community to visit periodically? List the people, tools and opportunities that will support you. Even if life seems quite manageable, activate your plan now, and it will be working for you when you most need it.

You might as well fall flat on your face
as lean over too far backward.
—James Thurber

Fostering Inner Balance

Inner balance in biology is known as dynamic equilibrium, a self-regulating process for maintaining stability while adjusting to changing conditions. Ideally, internal change continuously compensates for external change. In caregiving this inner balance is emotional. The adjustments and adaptations are made by you as you navigate the changeable emotional seas of your caregiving. As you practice inner balance by working to accept and adapt to change, you can find yourself confronted by your own fragility. Is balance, perhaps a simpler, more organic process than we imagine? I wrote in my diary:

> *My cat, with the immediacy of a thought, was up on the counter this morning. Just thought himself up there. Nature seems to happen that way, while we humanoids slog through mental mire. We weight ourselves with considerations. We are not proficient at living. When things go wildly out of balance, we struggle to right ourselves. Does nature worry about balance? Birds balance on branches but don't worry about it. It happens, or not, in which case they fly.*

One day, when walking with Mom, I noticed something interesting about balance. When she walked, she had to keep looking up to maintain her balance, but as I walked through caregiving I kept looking down, focusing only on the job that was directly in front of me so as to maintain control. It reminded me of yoga class. Like a person trying a yoga balance position for the first time, caregiving can be a wobbly experience. The harder you resist falling over, the more you falter. In yoga, the first instinct is to look down at your feet to block out any surrounding distractions, but then you lose your balance. The yoga master will tell you to look up at a distant point. When you can see where you fit in the broader picture, your perspective brings balance. It dawned on me that I could look up to broaden my view of caregiving, to see the bigger flow of events of which I was a part.

In the torturous dance between resistance and acceptance, a broad vision can be the key to balance and resilience. When you are new to this idea of accepting the moment, the tendency is to look down at your little particular piece of experience. As you become more adept, you will be able to look up to see the bigger picture of which you're a part. You are only a part. There is much you don't and can't know, and that is fine. You don't need all the answers.

A newspaper article on balance gives yet another insight. Philip Chard, in his article

Our Complaints Can Reveal a Path to Inner Balance (Milwaukee Journal Sentinel, July 14, 1998) talks about life being portrayed as a balancing act. He suggests that, "Leaning too far toward one extreme or another, whether in one's thoughts, emotions or behaviors, is fraught with the danger that one will take a psychological tumble. 'The golden mean' remains the time-tested method for keeping one's self poised on the high wire of existence rather than hurtling toward a hard landing." So, withholding extremes of emotion, or restraining oneself from extreme reactions, can be good advice during caregiving when we feel ourselves responding to extreme circumstances. Remaining self-contained within is a skill that lets you be more circumspect during apparent chaos.

Then again, getting through an off-balance time can be as simple as keeping your eyes on your goal and staying in motion. Sometimes when life with Mom felt out of kilter, my inspiration was a woman named Aggie. Aggie was the most off-kilter person I had ever known. In the face of her imbalance she stayed in motion. When I was a child she lived in the next block with her ancient father in a huge old house. In spite of having Parkinson's Disease, every day she took her dog for a walk. To keep her balance when walking she had to increase her speed, going faster and faster until something in her path stopped her. We would see her galloping past the bottom of our long cinder driveway, with her cocker spaniel doing its best to keep up.

One day Mom invited Aggie to come to tea. Aggie set out from her house with her thick wooden cane, loping faster and faster down the street and up our driveway to the front door and, crash! Aggie had arrived for tea. It must have taken guts to go out at all. A willingness to be unsure. An acceptance of the unknowns that faced her during every trip outside her front door. Aggie would choose her objective, set out, and stay in motion.

Remember to pause to see the breadth of your experience. Restrain yourself from indulging in extremes of emotion. And, like Aggie, keep your focus on the purpose that calls you forward. You will be in balance as you keep moving. Put one foot in front of the other and be thankful for each day, finding your equilibrium in the vision of yourself as a part of this great circle of life.

Respond to the following journaling prompts to clarify for yourself the meaning of balance.

Journaling Prompts on Balance

Turn to your caregiving journal and respond to the following:

1. When you find yourself feeling fragile or out of balance, stop and notice. Take a moment to write down a description of the feeling. Has your vision pulled in so that all you see is your little piece of the moment? Write about what you see. Write also about what you're not seeing.

2. In order to raise your vision, imagine the range of people and forces operating around you in your caregiving and in your life. Write about them. What is your place within that scene? Write about it. Do you feel a little calmer? Less fragile?

3. What are all of the forces (people, history, yourself) that have played and do play a part in your circumstances? What has brought you to this point in your life? What influences your days? How have these life factors colluded to give you your caregiving experience in the present?

4. Circle or highlight the factors over which you have no control. These are simply what is. Now write down a statement of caregiving goals, both for yourself and for others. What do you want to be true during caregiving? What are you determined will be true at the end of caregiving? Accept the things you cannot change and move forward, one day at a time.

Courage is fear that has said its prayers.
—Dorothy Bernard

Recharging Your Spirit

One definition of spirit is life force. We each have within us a life force. Aspects of caregiving can feel dispiriting. You may know spirit in its absence when you feel drained by grief, stress, or excessive empathizing. Perhaps someone in your life is undermining you. Loved ones can occasionally, with or without intention, sap your spirit. Caregiving is prime time for learning to protect, nurture and heal your spirit.

We have talked about maintaining connection with yourself during caregiving. Later in this chapter we will be talking about your ability to choose happiness. Both of these pertain to your relationship with yourself. The health of your spirit lives in the degree of connection between your inner spirit and the life force that is all around you. You may or may not think of this as God or your Higher Power, but spending time each day being present to it may bring you a peace that will sustain you.

Caroline E. Stephen, aunt of Virginia Woolf, in her book, *Quaker Strongholds*, tells us of her moment of peace during a Quaker meeting; "My whole soul was filled with the unutterable peace of the undisturbed opportunity for communion with God, with the sense that at last I had found a place where I might, without the faintest suspicion of insincerity, join with others in simply seeking His presence." For those of us for whom this force is not named God, this may translate more easily into sensing the presence of a life force, as in the unutterable peace of nature.

The book *Faith and Practice*, from the Society of Friends, broadens our vision, suggesting that people might find such unutterable peace "through group worship; through a relentless pursuit of truth; through a sense of the beauty and wonder of the world about them; through meditation; through art, music and literature; through sympathy and love in the family, and among their fellows."

Caregiving forced me daily to seek ways of healing my spirit. As I drove the ten miles to visit my mother in the nursing home, I would visualize a protective cloak around me, a barrier to the force of her negativity. Though I had never been one to pray, one day as I drove, I found myself spontaneously saying aloud, "Dear God, still my soul. Bring me thy peace. Give me a vision broad and blue to tent my day." Verbalizing this prayer gave me instant peace.

Certain locations or times of day can be conducive to connection with your life force.

My spirit is most alive in the early morning when I feel at one with nature. During caregiving, I began tentatively to dip my spiritual toe into the water of spontaneous prayer. I wrote:

> *Prayer is no passive beggarly state, but the active transmission of love to another, to the world, projecting pure healing. The more that's transmitted the more there is.*

In caregiving, the more I paid attention to the love all around me, the more available I was as a conduit of love in my life. As John Woolman tells us in his *Journal and Essays*, "The place of prayer is a precious habitation... I saw this habitation to be safe, to be inwardly quiet, when there was great stirrings and commotions in the world." Communing with the spirit makes everything a bit quieter, a bit easier. I gradually learned to choose life exactly as it was. Saying "Yes" to my life became one of my biggest tools for leveraging my well-being.

But then there were times when I just felt like quitting. In such moments, my prayers took on a more infantile tone:

> *I'd like to go away with God's blessing. I'd like Him, or someone, to clean up my life, saying, "You go on now. I'll take care of this mess and these people." So maybe I'm not a mountain climber after all. Maybe walking by the water in the valley will really make my cup run over.*

Wanting to seek relief or to take a break is so very human. You can make room for that feeling too. As you make room for your state of mind, whatever it is, and accept that you are merely a part of a much bigger whole, life gets easier.

You may need to set aside time to tune in to your spirit, or you may be able to do it moment by moment during the day. Whatever it takes, whatever it means to you, for the sake of everyone involved make spiritual recharging time a priority.

My Prayer of Acceptance

Listen here! I've done my best!
(Now I lay me down to rest)
I won't stop here but could this be...
(Where is thy staff to comfort me?)
Don't need to know what waits me there
(Be thou my comfort and support)
But keep me well. And keep me whole
(And after all, be still my soul.)

Now, take a moment to explore the meaning of spiritual healing for you.

JOURNALING PROMPTS ON SPIRITUAL HEALING

Turn to your caregiving journal and respond to the following:

1. Have there been ways, times, or places when you have been aware of a power greater than you? Where and when do you feel most spiritually alive? Jot down some words that describe your experience of each.

2. Write down where or from whom you have gotten your concepts of the presence of the spiritual, or its lack. Which version do you now endorse? Which, to you, seems to tell part of the story, but you feel there may be more to tell?

3. Whatever your faith of origin, what do God, spirit, prayer or meditation mean to you? What could they mean?

4. What would you need to change in your belief system, lifestyle, or daily schedule to allow for a regular spiritual practice?

This is your beginning because
you pack your own chute!
from the film "You Pack Your Own Chute"

PRACTICING SELF-CARE

Western culture values stoicism, and so teaches the puritanical ethic of toughing it out. This approach to life is ingrained in us as small children. In caregiving it can be a damaging way to live. You can only be as good for others as you have been good to yourself.

In caregiving, tending to your spiritual and physical health, like packing your own parachute, is an act of survival. The regular practice of self-care will foster the resilience that will carry you through caregiving.

I'm a natural skeptic who believes that anything is possible. There came a point in my caregiving when I knew that I needed all the help I could get. Alternative medicine became my mainstay. A regimen of alternative medicine practices can be a prime source of support for any caregiver. When checking out alternative medicine or the newer healing modalities, I double and triple check my sources. Fortunately, we live in a time when there are many tried and true options for alternative healing.

Even the National Institute of Health is recognizing the potential value of alternative medicine. The National Center for Complementary and Alternative Medicine (NCCAM, nccam.nih.gov) is the Federal Government's lead agency for scientific research on complementary and alternative medicine. It is one of the twenty-seven institutes and centers that make up the National Institutes of Health (NIH) within the U.S. Department of Health and Human Services.

Their mission is to:
- Explore complementary and alternative healing practices in the context of rigorous science.
- Train complementary and alternative medicine researchers.
- Disseminate authoritative information to the public and professionals.

Some approaches, such as Reiki, massage, and acupuncture, have such an impressive track record that they are used in hospitals. My daily regimen of healing techniques during caregiving kept me centered in myself and well rested. I use them still.

Yoga and massage are used widely to relieve anxiety. Both worked well for me. I attended yoga classes twice a week. It was a godsend! The stretching made me feel ten years younger. The breathing techniques even helped me to sleep through the night. These breathing and mind-focusing relaxation disciplines were invaluable for calming my over-active brain.

Massages were more than a delicious indulgence. They released the bad weather in my body, reminding my body and mind how to relax.

Reiki is a form of energy work that promotes physical healing and diminishes anxiety. (For information on research studies, visit the National Institute of Health webpage www.nih.gov and search for the term Reiki.) A one-day workshop can train you to self-administer treatments. Before becoming a certified Reiki practitioner, I took a day-long workshop called *Healing for Healers*. It was held in a sunlit cottage on top of a hill surrounded by 150 acres of fields. Twenty-five of us spent the day giving and receiving energy to and from each other. It was a struggle at first, because my back had been hurting badly. Halfway through the day I looked out the window to see a huge V of geese wheeling into view. They took six slow passes over the house before disappearing. The workshop leader said this sort of thing was common. She frequently had deer coming up to her windows or hundreds of wild turkeys landing outside her house. A friend of mine who had joined me for the workshop had a back which had been damaged in a series of accidents. Frequent pain was normal for her. She reported a few days later that her back had been feeling almost better ever since the workshop. My back also felt nearly perfect.

A few years into caregiving, I developed constant shoulder pain. My doctor was non-plussed. My chiropractor, usually a wonder-worker, couldn't address it. At that point I would have tried just about anything. I went to a local Integrative Therapist who practiced Self-guided Healing, a combination of Polarity, Neuro-linguistic Programming, and Craniosacral therapies. Her 1 1/2 hour session tapped into and healed childhood memories. By the end I felt physically and emotionally light, and my shoulders no longer hurt.

Of course, the most basic prescription for health and sleep is regular aerobic exercise. It releases endorphins into your system that are like happy pills. Walk with a friend and have a chat. Bring an iPod and listen to an uplifting lecture or music.

Make your self-care a personal treat. Open yourself to new approaches. By making self-care a priority, you will set yourself up for doing your best as a caregiver.

Use the following journal questions to help you to incorporate self-care practices into your lifestyle.

JOURNALING PROMPTS ON SELF-CARE

Turn to your caregiving journal and respond to the following:

1. What alternative healing practice, exercise, or health regimen might you enjoy and be willing to do routinely? Some take only a few moments to get a result. Run a search on-line and make notes about the ones that most appeal to you.

2. Whom do you know that would be a good resource for information or referral for local practitioners or resources? Who might be a good buddy with whom you could practice?

3. Notice the thoughts running through your head as you consider these alternatives. Write down your stories about alternative medicine or health regimens that may present obstacles to moving forward.

4. Rank the possibilities on your list according to their appeal. Start by adding one new practice to your week right now, the one to which you are most drawn. Then, after a few weeks, try adding another. You'll know when you have enough.

Each morning when I open my eyes
I say to myself: 'I, not events, have the power
to make me happy or unhappy today.'
—Groucho Marx

Choosing Happiness

We speak of emotions as though we are their victims. We relinquish free choice by succumbing to easy phrases—The news "makes me" so upset! You're "driving me" crazy! This "makes me" so sad! But you have more say about your happiness than you think. You think that your words describe your real emotional truth but what if, as we have said, words are magic? How might they be creating the world of our emotions? Let's have a quick review: Most of us live as though:

1. First "reality" happens. Someone says or does something.
2. That creates an emotion in you.
3. And then you describe it.

But what if our emotions arise like this:

1. You choose a word (such as sadness or fear) to describe some change in your body (a sinking feeling, or a tension for instance.)
2. But it is the word that then evokes, or causes, the emotion.
3. That word-sourced feeling is then cemented in place as your reality, your experience.

About five years ago, I was asked to speak to the Presbytery of Northern New England as a member of a Presbyterian Peace and Justice committee. My knees were so weak that I knew I would not be able to walk to the podium. But then I noticed that what I had named "fear" actually felt, in the pit of my stomach, remarkably like excitement. I switched the story I was telling myself, and began to tell myself that I was excited. I noticed that excitement is an outward-moving emotion, while fear had felt like an inward-turning. As I rose and successfully walked to the podium, I focused on directing my excitement outward to support and strengthen my voice. I was later told that I had seemed completely self-possessed, had spoken calmly and clearly.

This simple act of naming a feeling that serves you better gives you room to choose a different response. Like a child playing in the costume chest, you can try on different interpretations of what is happening.

An alternative to changing your thinking about a troublesome circumstance is to change the circumstance. Many times, you can choose to remove yourself altogether from a problem situation. If the daily news is distressing to you, take a moratorium. The world will not end. Whatever you find to be upsetting in a given moment, ask yourself, *What are my options here? What am I missing? What's another way of seeing or dealing with this?* Then make the choice that sustains your spirit.

Surely you know of activities and people that make you happier. I love my solitude and, given our history, my connection with Mom was too close for comfort, especially at first. Yet I re-chose our connection every day. But even after a good day with her, getting in my car and driving away was a relief. The movement of my car uplifted me. Movement of any kind was therapeutic. As my chiropractor says, "Life is movement, and movement is life." Journaling, Reiki, and massage all released me, moving my energy, relaxing tension. And I worked every day at choosing my happiness to keep my resilience.

One fall I gave myself a real break. I went on a silent weekend retreat at the home of a Quaker friend. Charlotte Fardelman (author of *Nudged by the Spirit*) lives in a charming old home on the bay between Portsmouth, NH and the island of New Castle. Her broad lawn sloping down to the water was a spectacular setting for reflecting on life. Bless her for sharing it with her friends. I wrote and wrote.

> *This middle age isn't about knowing at all, but about letting go, emptying out, getting down to the lowest common denominator that divides any sorrow, confusion, or pain. Staying open to unexpected moments, unplanned outcomes, unenvisioned gifts. Giving up knowing in favor of being. The doing follows from being.*

My inner work was making it all right. I was gaining the power to decide how to relate to my life. I was gaining the tools for leveraging my well-being and happiness.

Choose to manage your emotions, create the conditions for happiness, and you will mitigate the emotional toll taken by caregiving. It is an empowering realization. You need not be so much at the sway of events.

Take a minute to reflect on your own conditions for happiness by journaling with the following questions.

JOURNALING PROMPTS ON HAPPINESS

Turn to your caregiving journal and respond to the following:

1. When, where, or with whom are you most happy? Why? Write down what it is about certain places and people that makes you happy. Which of these could you add more of to your days? List them.

2. List the activities or experiences that drain you of energy. Why do you do them? What is your motivation? Make notes beside each one. Let's say you are doing something that drains you, and the motivation is loyalty. What other actions motivated by loyalty could you take that would *give* you energy?

3. What does the way you speak about feelings reveal about your beliefs and their source? Write down a few statements of strong feeling. If I said, "I feel so angry around him—he makes me feel so small" my words could reveal that I am giving "him" a lot of power. How would this feel different? "I don't like who I am around him. I am not, by nature, a small person. I have choices."

4. Do you see some new options or choices available to you, either by shifting your beliefs or by changing your circumstances? In the example above, could I intentionally choose to feel bigger when I know I'm going to see "him?" Each shift you make moves you toward happiness.

To truly laugh, you must be able to
take your pain and play with it.
—Charlie Chaplin

USING HUMOR

This may sound contradictory but, since caregiving is serious business, don't overlook the well-being value of humor. I'm serious. Not only does it mitigate times of tension, it plays a therapeutic role. Humor helps to move you through your emotional terrain. It is deeply healing on many levels.

Norman Cousins, in his book *Anatomy of an Illness,* describes how he used laughter to cure himself of chronic illness. He had been given one chance in 500 of surviving an inflammation of the connective tissue. He could barely move. He decided, among other things, to act on the theory that humor is healing. A movie projector was delivered to his hospital room, and he began watching Candid Camera films and old Marx Brothers movies sent to him by his friend, comedian Allen Funt. The nurse read aloud to him, especially from E.B. and Katharine White's *Subtreasury of American Humor,* and Max Eastman's *The Enjoyment of Laughter.*

The measure of his illness was the rate of sedimentation of his blood. They took readings of his sedimentation rate before and after laughter sessions, finding that each time the numbers had dropped at least five more points, and that was cumulative day to day. Ten minutes of laughter relieved his pain, allowing him to sleep for two hours at a stint. He recovered fully, subsequently living a long and healthy life —well into his 80's! He believed that his own laughter cured his disease.

When you are under stress, your body produces Cortisol, the fight or flight hormone. Your blood pressure spikes. Your immune system and heart are stressed. Laughter significantly reduces your levels of Cortisol. Patrick A. McGuire, in an American Psychological Association article entitled *More Psychologists Are Finding That Discrete Uses of Humor Promote Healing in Their Patients* (www.apa.org/monitor/mar99) tells us that "Medical experts have already demonstrated that laughter boosts the immune system increasing natural disease-fighting killer cells and lowering blood pressure."

Humor is not only like a little vacation for the emotions, it helps to move you through those emotions. In caregiving I found black humor to be especially effective. It's a short leap from tears to laughter. Emotions released (rather than dwelt upon) are healing. Imagine what would happen if you introduced more humor into your relationship with your loved one?

My mom had a sense of delicacy about bodily functions. In rehab her dignity quickly went out the window. When the aides would come to help her in the bathroom we joked about it, saying, "For heavens sake! Leave the woman what's left of her dignity!" We laughed in the face of surreal moments.

For me, I always thought of each day as a new day. A friend had given me a little bag of cotton and beads that was labeled Possibilities. I hung it beside the kitchen door. Each time I left the house, I'd give it a good long squeeze. Then it began to remind me of a body part. I'd give a little inner shriek and a chuckle, and start my day.

I even invented ways to laugh on demand. As I drove on errands I would think of old croony love songs and then sing them... to myself!... in an Elmer Fudd voice as though they were love songs to Me. Yes, I sang love songs to myself. Whatever works! Try it. Sing in a quavering voice, "Fwy me to de moooon" and see if you don't start to titter. Or, "I wuv oooo faw sentimental weasons." I laughed till I *cwied* and almost went off the *woad*.

Ed Dunkleblau, Ph.D believes that humor is much more than simply therapeutic. Dunkleblau is a consultant who gives training sessions to therapists on using humor in treatment. He says of humor, "It's not a therapy. It's a complementary treatment. It facilitates that which we do as therapists. We're trying to help people problem-solve, to develop, to know they're alive. These are things that humor does."

So stock up on comedy films and prescribe one whenever you need it. Introduce doses of humor into your daily routine with your loved one. It will be good for both of you. Keep reminding yourself, *If I don't take care of myself I'm no good to anyone.* Every step you take to keep your spirit up is an essential act in your caregiving. Make the time to think and act in your own best interest, for the sake of everyone involved.

Now play for a moment with how and where you might access some humor to lighten up your caregiving by answering the following questions.

JOURNALING PROMPTS ON HUMOR

Turn to your caregiving journal and respond to the following:

1. What situations make you laugh? Do you love stupid comedies? Have you recently developed a funny bone for black humor? It's okay to be "a little twisted" if it gives you uplift. List some ways that you could give yourself a daily dose of humor.

2. Make a list of the people who make you laugh. Which ones could you visit or phone each week?

3. Who in your life, in the final analysis, is a downer? Who takes more energy than they give? If possible, limit time spent with them to a minimum.

4. Make a list of the activities or places that sap your good humor, like watching the news, or visiting a certain relative. Note beside each whether you could take a moratorium, or at least experience it less frequently.

In this chapter we explored ways of being good to yourself by building self-connection and inner balance, recharging your spirit, and practicing self-care. We looked at the complex necessity of asking for help, and the possibility of using humor and choosing happiness.

In the next chapter you will see how to use what you have learned so far in a number of ways to greatly improve your effectiveness as a caregiver.

RESOURCES

Books

I Never Knew I Had a Choice: Explorations in Personal Growth, by Gerald Corey

The Artist's Way, by Julia Cameron

Everyday You: Create Your Day with Joy and Mindfulness, by Eric Maisel

The Architecture of Happiness, by Alain De Botton

A Thousand Names for Joy: Living in Harmony with the Way Things Are, by Byron Katie

Mindfulness of Breathing: Managing Pain, Illness, and Stress with Guided Mindfulness Meditation, by Sona and Vidyamala

Subtreasury of American Humor , by E.B. and Katharine White

The Enjoyment of Laughter., by Max Estman

Connections, by Gabrielle Roth

Magazines & Websites

Body & Soul www.wholeliving.com

Going Bonkers www.gbonkers.com

Inner Change www.innerchangemag.com

Tathaastu : So Be It www.tathaastumag.com

Soulful Living www.soulfulliving.com

Chicago Tribune Health Blog www.featuresblogs.chicagotribune.com

Empowering Caregivers www.care-givers.com

CHAPTER SIX

APPLYING THE PRINCIPLES
TO YOUR EFFECTIVENESS

We have an internal system operating constantly
which determines the results we get in our lives.
Until we intimately understand our results system,
we will feel at the effect of life and circumstance.
—Sydney Rice-Harrild, author of *Choice Points*

What if your chief obstacles to being more effective in caregiving are primarily inside of yourself, so close that they are invisible to you? If that is true, you will need to find a way to see them before you can deal with them. Your personal history has defined much of your role within your world. Your personality, in effect, runs you, offering a restricted viewpoint and set of options. To maximize your effectiveness, you will need a broader viewpoint. You will need to step out of your box.

In this chapter we will uncover your automatic role as a caregiver so that you can choose a more useful way of being. You will reveal and then fine-tune your commitments. You will identify the battles in your caregiving, and then learn to pick battles carefully in order to sustain forward motion. Awareness of your voice as a child, mother, or partner will free you to shift that voice. Attention to habitual acts of survival will make useful strategies available. Clarity about your relationship with your loved one's medical team could save the day. Step by step, you will clarify who you want to be as a caregiver.

Life is full of internal dramas, instantaneous and
sensational, played to an audience of one.
—Anthony Powell

PICKING YOUR BATTLES

But restraining a readiness to do battle can be like breaking a bad habit. Not only do some of us have well-defended natures, our culture supports our on-guard stance. In many arenas of life we are encouraged to defend our rights, distrust the establishment, and complain about the state of the world. When there are no new outer battles to wage, we wage inner ones. During caregiving, if you wage battles indiscriminately you give away your energy. What would happen to your battles if you stayed present, spoke or thought in new ways, and practiced acceptance?

Picking Your Battles, by Bonnie Maslin, gives us a few valuable preliminary considerations. Though it was written for parents coping with parenting, its wisdom is equally useful for caregivers. She tells us, "Not all battles are well waged or worthwhile. More often than not, battles resolve little they seem intended to address, and instead get endlessly replayed. All too often they make things worse." She wisely suggests that you need to understand "which battles are necessary and how to wage them adaptively... to make anger work for, rather than against, you." She then proposes Four Key Steps for Preventing Unnecessary Battles:

1. Set reasonable expectations
2. Develop a common sense philosophy
3. Create thoughtful and practical policy
4. Adopt a positive pattern... by eliminating self-defeating "No-win Discipline Reactions."

As Ms. Maslin implies, battles often arise due to unexamined expectations. Life doesn't always measure up, and when it doesn't we feel something on the continuum from disappointment to frustration to total exasperation. I learned from my exasperation as I wrote in my diary

I hurt when I hope. I have expectations but they end up having me... for dinner. I am eaten alive by the expectations of others and my expectations of them.

Ultimately the world does not have to go your way. You can play your part and then let go, releasing the situation to evolve. Wage war adaptively. As you let go of the expectations that give rise to outrage, you will be freed to see the bigger picture. The smoke will clear.

You can speak your truth with calm authority because you haven't compromised your inner strength with unnecessary upset.

Opportunities for doing battle popped up daily when I returned to caregiving after my cancer surgery. Mom had restrained herself while I was incapacitated by chemo, but when I returned I got an earful. The nursing home manager was determined that her facility would not have the usual nursing home smell and ambiance. Not a bad ambition. She kept the place spotless, but she also forbade residents from sitting in the sun room. She thought it didn't look well. It also soon became clear that the doctor and kitchen staff were oblivious to the connection between diet and health. Opportunities for upset abounded. One day I stopped, stood still, and noticed (was present to the fact) that my agitation was causing more problems than it was solving.

Two decades earlier I, a meek Quaker, had worked for the nuns of a small conservative Catholic women's college. Curiously, my boss was a man, whose deep, bemused voice I can still hear telling me, "You have to pick your battles." That became one of my caregiving mantras, along with the phrase, "There is no emergency." That way of thinking allowed me to wage only the bigger battles, giving up the small skirmishes. I recognized my primary purpose to be making time with Mom as pleasant as possible. That became my practical policy.

Then there are the inner battles. When it came time for me to leave Mom's room she would plead with me, "Don't go. Don't leeeave me. I neeeeed you!" My first instinct was to lay down the law—"No more pleading!" —thereby enforcing what Ms. Maslin would call a self-defeating no-win discipline reaction. But then, caught between my own needs and my discomfort with confronting her, I had a flash of insight. I centered myself and asked myself, *What way of speaking would Mom be able to hear?* She was my mother. I knew she cared about my well-being, so I adapted by speaking out of that knowledge. I told her that her pleading made it harder for me to partner with her. I asked her to help both of us by freeing me to go home to take care of myself. She was always big on me taking care of myself, so she could hear that.

When you find yourself battling the way someone speaks to you, stop with compassion and ask yourself what response they would be able to hear. A new resolution may show up. Picking battles does not mean bottling up your feelings or keeping under wraps your insights into how to improve things. It does mean treading carefully, with a discerning eye toward what is important. Knowing the source of your upset will allow you to take appropriate action.

The following exercise will help you to differentiate between your issues, dispense with the lesser ones, and tackle only those that are worthy of battle.

How To Pick Your Battles

Step One: Identify Your Expectations

1. Choose a current issue. (If you can only think of one from the past, pretend that it is happening now. You'll want to see how this works so that you can use it later.) Write down a detailed description of it including who is involved, what you think of them or the situation, what you feel about the issue, what you believe is true about every aspect of it.

2. Underline the words you have used that imply assumptions or expectations. Watch for the use of words such as Is, Are, Was, Couldn't, Should, Must, and Didn't. They point to what you assert to be true. Watch for words that point to interpretations, like Seemed, or Acted Like.

3. Then on a separate page, list the assumptions or expectations you see that you have held in regard to yourself, someone else, caregiving, or life in general.

Step Two: Clarify the Degree of Urgency

1. List up to six important caregiving tasks, issues, or challenging conversations that face you.

2. With your caregiving goals in mind, rate each on a scale from 1 to 5 with "Critical" at one end and "No Big Deal" at the other. How much energy does each deserve?

3. About the ones that carry some urgency ask yourself the following questions: Can this be changed? (Hint: You can't change other people.) Is it appropriately mine to handle? Is this issue critical to my caregiving objectives? Is there another way of seeing this that would diminish its urgency?

4. By now you will have identified the non-critical issues, the ones that you truly don't have to address. Cross them off the first list and put them on a separate list labeled DECOMMITMENTS.

5. On a separate page write the truly critical issues, leaving plenty of space below each. These are the ones that are a threat to health, safety or the peace of mind of you or a loved one. (The remaining non-critical issues can be dispatched one each day, starting with the easiest or most important. Get help or delegate when possible.)

STEP THREE: ENGAGE IN BATTLE

1. Below each of the critical issues, write your assumptions and expectations using the process in Step One: Identify Your Expectations.

2. As you consider the people involved, your desired outcome, and your caregiving goals, do any new adaptive creative solutions come to mind?

3. Note what would need to happen in order to get each issue handled. What is required? By whom?

4. Whose buy-in would be helpful? List any other assistance that might be necessary or desirable for each.

5. Make requests. Hire help. If you need help but are unclear how to get it, brainstorm with a trusted friend or professional.

6. If a more complete conversation is necessary, design it carefully. Speak respectfully. If necessary, make promises (not threats) on which you can and would follow through.

7. If the issue has not been solved and is still urgent, then escalate it. Bring it step-by-step to higher authorities. For instance, if your issue is with a nursing home employee, the chain of command may be the Director of Nursing, the Administrator, and then your Ombudsman.

To increase your effectiveness,
make your emotions subordinate to your commitments
—Brian Koslow

DRIVING RESULTS WITH COMMITMENTS

Most of us engage in our days oblivious to our commitments, yet they steer us, inciting us to action. First let me clarify what I mean by commitment. Commitment is stronger than a responsibility or desire. A commitment is a course of action, belief or value to which you choose to be bound. At work we may have commitments to not rock the boat, to look good to the boss, or steadily to advance. At home our commitments may include keeping the kids safe, having an attractive house, or getting attention from our spouse.

On most days these commitments chug us along, generating the life that we think we want, but difficulty arises when we simultaneously hold conflicting commitments. Living with unrecognized conflicting commitments leaves you feeling disturbed or on the fence, and you probably won't know why. A client of mine was feeling constant stress over her tug-of-war with her aging mother. During a coaching session, she recognized her conflicting commitments; to be a good caregiver, and to be her mother's friend. Once she saw the stalemate and reordered her commitments, she felt great freedom. Then, in any given moment, she was free consciously to choose her appropriate role.

My first conflicting caregiving commitments existed on a primal level. I began caregiving with my typical stoic determination and good cheer, but as Mom began to decline, I increasingly felt bewildered by the enormity of the unknowns, numb at the thought of heading into this wilderness with a woman I had long avoided. My conflict arose from being committed both to helping my mother, and to staying safe. I was stuck in a very uncomfortable place. I needed to delve more deeply into my commitments to myself, to my mother, and to caregiving.

To clarify my commitments, I first visualized my best outcomes, which were:
- My time with Mom will redeem our history;
- I will emerge from it emotionally whole; and
- I will have my sisters in my life.

From that visualization flowed my caregiving commitments, some of which conflicted or shifted in priority as I went forward. Having listed my best outcomes, I was able to see clearly my commitments to my mother, my family, and myself. Whenever I felt unsure about what action to take, I asked myself, *What is my primary commitment here?* Identifying your commitments and defining them out of your vision for the future, rather than out of reaction to your past, is a powerful step on your road to power and peace.

By contrast, there are times when you know exactly what is true, what action should be taken, and you will sacrifice a good deal to prove yourself right. But an inflexible need to be right closes down your options, shutting down relationships. Taken to the extreme, rigid fixation on your one truth is a painful way to live—life becomes a choice between being right or being happy. If this strikes a chord with you, you're not alone.

When I asked my sisters for help, I was feeling isolated. I needed to know who would be supporting me and in what ways. I was astonished at my one sister's unexplained refusal to phone me. Then I was outraged. Then I looked at my pre-stated commitment regarding sisters. I said to myself, *You can be right, OR you can keep this sister in your life.* If I had continued self-righteously judging her I would have disowned her.

A more ordinary alternative to personal outrage is suppressing emotions, but that is never healthy. It also doesn't move us to new ground. It closes down possibilities. Health issues aside, by repressing feelings we lose opportunities for growth and enriched relationships. So what would be a healthy life-affirming alternative? Answering that will take a little more rooting around and reflection. When conflicting commitments fuel anger, there often lurks a questionable assumption. Assumptions drive the story you tell yourself about life. They are the story behind the story.

The assumption that gave rise to my anger was that my sister would be there for me in a prescribed way. When I saw that, I realized that my definition of "sister" needed to broaden. I had to expand my assumptions to make room for who my sister really was. Perhaps she was doing the best that she could given her own limitations. I decided to be grateful for the support she *was* able to give. A few times a year she brought Mom up for a visit with her for a few days, or popped in for family celebrations. And every couple of years she pitched in to help with one of Mom's moves.

Keep an on-going list of your commitments based on a vision of your future rather than your past. Then allow for the power that is available in flexibility. Be willing to consider new options and perspectives. As you shift your assumptions about what must happen, opportunities will arise to reshape your story about what is true. You have far more leeway than you originally thought.

Now let's continue your personal exploration by seeing how you might apply these principles to a specific incident in your life. Answer the following questions to see what new viewpoint might present itself.

JOURNALING PROMPTS ON COMMITMENTS

Turn to your caregiving journal and respond to the following:

1. Think of a recent experience that didn't go well for you. It might have been a conversation, or the way you handled a caregiving situation, or it might just have been a time when you felt yourself strongly resisting an aspect of caregiving. Write down a brief description.

2. Ask yourself, *What am I telling myself is true about this situation?* Write down everything that you felt is true about what happened, the people involved, and the way it played out.

3. Ask yourself, *What are my commitments in this situation, to myself and to others?* Each point of upset will reveal a commitment or two. You wouldn't be upset if you weren't committed to something. Write down whatever comes to mind without editing your responses.

4. Finally, look through your answers to the first three questions and write down any assumptions that you see underlying your scenario. These could be assumptions about people, about the human race, about what is right, just, or fair. Write some alternate ways to think about each.

When I serve, I see and trust (an other's) wholeness.
It is what I am responding to and collaborating with.
—Rachel Naomi Remen

DEFINING YOUR ROLE

A common ethic goes something like, "Helping is good." It ain't necessarily so. This naively simple cultural assumption sidesteps a somewhat intricate set of considerations. Perhaps you're thinking, *How complex can this be? Caregivers simply want to help.* Well, yes, but some common forms of "helping" can be not only inappropriate, they can be disempowering to your loved one. While many of us have experience as helpers or fixers, few of us truly understand the powerfully healing action of service. Greater clarity about your role as a caregiver can focus you on exactly the kind of "helper" *you* want to be in caregiving.

Rachel Naomi Remen is the Clinical Professor of Family and Community Medicine at the UCSF School of Medicine, and author of *Kitchen Table Wisdom: Stories That Heal.* In her essay, *In the Service of Life,* she spells out the difference between fixing, helping, and serving. Her message is a powerful guide for the effective caregiver.

Dr. Remen distinguishes between serving and helping by pointing out that helping is rooted in inequality. The focus is on the other person as someone who is weaker and more needy. She then distinguishes between serving and fixing, saying that fixing implies that the other person is broken. In service, you see the wholeness of the other, and then partner with that wholeness. Fixing comes from a judging mentality, which creates disconnection and distance. Serving only happens when we are intimately connected with those we serve. As Mother Teresa tells us, we serve life not because it is broken but because it is holy. Finally, Dr. Remen speaks to the inner experience of serving. Though helping, fixing and serving can look alike to the observer, the inner experiences differ. Over time, fixing and helping are draining, while service is renewing. When we serve, our work sustains us.

As many caregivers do, I learned the hard way. I began caregiving as both a helper and a fixer, but I wouldn't let anyone help me. I began to feel used up, like a little bit of gray soap in life's soap dish. I was then diagnosed with colon cancer, which put me out of circulation for six months. As I lay in bed healing, I was told that Mom was doing just fine without me. Well sure, she did have professionals looking after her. But then Mom proudly reported to me how she was managing her life, doing things I had previously been handling. She was paying her own bills, writing checks with her crippled hand, communicating with the management of the nursing home, and ordering Christmas presents by phone for the family. My "help" had been disempowering her.

What determines the balance between self-care and nurturing others? How much of my helping was I doing just to make myself feel better? How could I support without taking over? Give without giving myself away? Behind my battle-ready approach to mother-care was not only a mistaken idea of the meaning of help, I had also made the false assumption that it was all up to me.

We, as caregivers, feel ourselves to be in a position of responsibility. The way we take the lead, proactively designing our caregiving, can have the quality of serving. The phrase "Servant Leadership" was coined by Robert K. Greenleaf in *The Servant as Leader*, an essay first published in 1970. As you read this excerpt from his essay, hold his message within the context of caregiving and see if it doesn't ring true:

> "The servant-leader is servant first… It begins with the natural feeling that one wants to serve, to serve first. Then conscious choice brings one to aspire to lead. That person is sharply different from one who is leader first, perhaps because of the need to assuage an unusual power drive… The leader-first and the servant-first are two extreme types. Between them there are shadings and blends that are part of the infinite variety of human nature."

> "The difference manifests itself in the care taken by the servant-first to make sure that other people's highest priority needs are being served. The best test, and difficult to administer, is: Do those served grow as persons? Do they, while being served, become healthier, wiser, freer, more autonomous?"

In order to foster autonomy in everyone involved, I switched to thinking of me and my mom as partners. I explicitly spoke to Mom of our time together as a partnership. When we were effectively partnering, I pointed it out. I let my husband contribute by being a second pair of ears for me, a second pair of hands. Our marriage became a training ground in partnering. I invited him to be my advocate, ensuring that I took care of myself. Together, we explored what it could mean to listen without judging, to give advice only by permission. We learned to partner in service. I needed and had a right to manage my life with Mom on my terms, but he could support me in that. And Mom had a right to manage her own life as long as she could. He was in service to me, while I was in service to Mom. We had a triangle of service. Life came to be about mastery, not control.

Use the following questions to explore your caregiver role, as it is, and as it could be.

JOURNALING PROMPTS ON YOUR ROLE

Turn to your caregiving journal and respond to the following:

1. Make notes about who taught you about giving, your role models. What are the "truths" that you learned? What, to you, are generosity, help, service, and martyrdom?

2. Write down people you have known who are/were truly "in service." What qualities or personal style did they exhibit? Describe their voices, the kinds of questions they asked, or statements they made. What about their demeanor told you that they were serving either you or someone else?

3. Write down some of the ways and the people with whom you have functioned as a helper or a fixer. In what aspects of your caregiving might you switch to serving your loved one? In what situations could you better respond to her/his wholeness?

4. What kind of service would you like to request for yourself and from whom? Whom do you experience as trying to help or fix you? How might you teach them to serve you on your terms? What would those terms be? Write down your personal definition of service, the kind that you would like to receive. Be specific. For you to feel served, who would need to do what?

Habit is the enormous flywheel of society,
its most precious conservative agent.
—William James

MOVING FROM SURVIVING TO THRIVING

As you enter caregiving, life can at first look familiar. But, like Alice stepping through the looking glass, it will begin to respond differently. Relationships can move to a new footing. Expectations will change. The set routines and communication patterns established early on can help to stabilize you throughout caregiving. And when things get turbulent, peacemaking tactics from the past can restore some stability.

From day one, I set my routine with Mom, and for ten years I spent two days a week with her. (Periodic health problems at times required daily visits.) She and I both counted on the regularity of the routine. I needed to know there was a limit to my giving. She needed to know what she could count on. In a time when so much was changing, the weekly schedule was a comforting solid element. And when things got off track, historic tactics for bringing peace were a mainstay.

At first, we ran errands, shared tea in her sunny living room, and lunched in the formal dining room of her retirement community. Occasionally, Mom drove her car to our house for dinner, but she wasn't invited as often as she would have liked. She reminded John of his nasty alcoholic father—within the first ten minutes of a visit, she would begin criticizing some aspect of our home. So she and I kept to ourselves. Our time together was made up of known quantities. But, as it was to happen every place that Mom lived, after only a few months in that first community the blush faded. In the dining room she grew disgusted by the way the other "inmates" ate. Their conversation was "inane." No one had attended a "decent" college. As her unhappiness insinuated itself into emerging cracks in my pleasant veneer, I turned to ways of de-fusing tense moments that I had developed years ago.

Dad was a good Quaker, but an oppressive upbringing had taught him the art of passive aggression—he teased Mom. His tactics, bothersome as peas under her mattress, niggled until she exploded. I always knew exactly when Mom had gone over the edge. She would plunk herself down on the kitchen floor, pull all the pots, pans and lids out of the drawers into a big crashing pile, and she would laugh. Not a happy laugh, but a crazed witchy laugh. Then Mom would be ready for a drive. She and I loved getting lost. We would head out, taking random turns. We'd wander for a couple of hours, commenting on the scenery and getting out of ourselves. Eventually, we'd see a familiar street name or route number. We always managed to get home.

Some twenty-five years later, Mom and I called upon on that old strategy to relieve new tensions, driving the winding roads of New Hampshire in all weathers. But then there came a time when I needed to step beyond the familiar strategies.

Sydney Rice-Harrild, life coach and author of *Choice Points*, speaks to the critical transition from the old strategies to the new approaches: "For the most part, your historic ways of operating can stand you in good stead. When all hell starts breaking loose, taking a few moments to notice what has worked in the past. Old interpersonal behaviors or solutions can quickly put you on familiar territory. You already have them to pull from. Though later you will need to step out and try new approaches, for now these will be a comfort."

For now. What is there, for you, beyond "for now?" What is it that will have you need to try new approaches? What will you do when historic ways of operating immerse you deeper in trouble? Remember the case of the boiling frog in Chapter One. When you find yourself in familiar water that is getting hotter, how do you jump?

These are the times when, as therapist/author Tommy Hellsten, says, "True strength can only be found in weakness." New circumstances will call on you for strengths as yet undiscovered. The first is to acknowledge your weakness, and yet jump to unfamiliar ground. In order to move to this new ground successfully, you will need to let go, to experience your vulnerability in order to open to your newly emerging strengths.Mr. Hellsten explains, "Truth lives within us, often deeper than our rational understanding. When we listen to this truth, we often doubt ourselves, even though we are headed in the right way. True growth requires that we listen to our innermost self rather than to our limited understanding."

Growth is an evolution, starting with where you are, then moving (or leaping) to new ground. In the process, you learn to trust yourself. Ideally, as in the previous section on Inner Balance, internal change continuously compensates for external change.

Learn early in caregiving to utilize time-tested routines and tactics for rebalancing that will help you and your loved one retain greater normalcy. Then, when you are faced with shifting circumstances, remember the boiling frog. Caregiving doesn't stay predictable for long, but you have deep intuitions you can learn to trust to take you into new territory, to build new strength and strategies. Between the known elements you have in place, and the new ones you invent, you will more easily move through caregiving.

Use the following questions to take a closer look at your life-saving routines and tactics. Write them in your journal so that they will be there for you when you need them. Also write about your ability to find new strengths and strategies.

JOURNALING PROMPTS ON SURVIVAL TACTICS

Turn to your caregiving journal and respond to the following:

1. When and how, in the past, have you felt most connected to your loved one? Can you see in your history with her/him, or with others, familiar ways of relieving tension that might now be useful? Make a "Tension Reliever" list. Then note how each idea could be adapted during caregiving. Also note any new ideas that may crop up in the process.

2. What degree of contact is your loved one requesting? Do you feel you ought to visit more often than might be good for you, your loved one, or your family? Make some notes here. Who generates the "ought-to's" in your life? What could be the cost to everyone of visiting too much? What ideal schedule could you commit to for the future?

3. Think back to a time in the past when you handled a crisis or challenge with surprising creativity or strength. What was your experience? Who did you have to be in order to improve the situation? What were the new strengths that you found in yourself?

4. Looking at your caregiving now, is there a situation that is calling for a more creative response than your usual ones? What might a new approach look like? What does your intuition suggest? Are you open to considering all possible actions, including doing nothing?

Never ignore a gut feeling,
but never believe that it's enough.
—Robert Heller

ADVOCATING EFFECTIVELY

Keeping watch over your loved one while maintaining warm relations with medical staff is an art. It is not uncommon to feel afraid of offending those whose good will has an impact on a loved one's well-being. It can feel like a double bind. The path between keeping the peace and being your loved one's advocate can seem, at times, a narrow one. I wrote in my diary:

I want to believe that I'm doing what I can. Don't want to rock the boat, to turn anyone against me. I need these nurses and aides. It's hard to know what to do, or refrain from doing. Where's the line over which I shouldn't step? The doctor says that we're doing what needs to be done. Are we?

How do you see your relationship with your loved one's medical team? You probably don't want to make waves, yet it's a good idea to be watchful. It can be easy, when vulnerable, to want the comfort of implicit trust in a doctor. Yes, trust is a necessary piece of the doctor/client relationship, but let it be an informed trust. Learn about medical testing and the interactions between medications. Study the doctor's decision-making style. How does (s)he work? Think about the aspects of caregiving that place new demands on a physician/client relationship.

The mother of a client of mine had a nursing home doctor who was charming, but as her health issues became increasingly more critical, the doctor responded only minimally. My client, Janet, felt the need to trust him. She and her mother didn't want another crisis. Janet told me, "He's the doctor. Shouldn't I believe that he knows best?" Even after the nurse thrust Ombudsman brochures into her hand saying, "You have rights!" she was slow to take action. She told me that she felt at the mercy of the nursing home's good will. Two trips to the hospital from misdiagnoses had her finally acknowledge that there was a problem. We talked over various possible courses of action. She finally documented the recent series of events and took the notes to the head of nursing. From then on, though Janet felt timid and unsure, we worked on her trusting her intuition. Whenever her intuitive red flag went up, we talked about actions she could take. There were times to ask for clarification, and other times to press hard for second opinions and testing. Throughout this period, Janet stepped up her own self-care to help her cope with the stress. Finally, with a change in treatment, the mother's confusion, (which Janet had been told was normal in the elderly,) cleared up. Life stabilized.

Intuition, backed by information, can be your mainstay as you advocate for your loved one. Educate yourself so that you can interpret what is happening. An elder's body responds quite differently from ours to a variety of factors. They are more sensitive to changes in medications and to changes in their environment. A move to or from the hospital or a urinary tract infection (UTI) can make them temporarily lose touch with reality. Prescribing meds for the elderly is a ticklish business. Their often large collections of prescriptions must be delicately balanced to avoid conflicts between drugs. But while caution in medicating the elderly is wise, some old-style doctors can be slow to prescribe the meds necessary to stave off crisis. Know the doctor.

However well-meaning the medical team, mistakes can happen. Nursing is a complex business. Professionals don't go into healthcare because it is fun or lucrative—they are in it to help people. The hours are long, lives may be at stake, and everyone is emotionally challenged. At a nursing home or hospital, medical staff must keep families happy, residents healthy, and government red tape in order. Family members are under stress, perhaps hyper-alert to any perceived slip in the care of their loved one. Ideally these doctors, aides and nurses are your caregiving partners. Though they may not always be as efficient as you would like, it can serve you from the outset to assume that they are doing their very best.

If you are lacking information or understanding, ask questions, as many as necessary to have your finger on the pulse of your loved one's treatment.. Any good professional should welcome respectful reasonable questions. Be gracious whenever possible.

Keep a medical diary and a watchful steady eye. If you see something you don't like, ask yourself, *Is this critical? Could it impact my loved one's wellbeing or health?* If the answer is yes, speak out respectfully and directly. If it continues, escalate the issue up the management chain. Trust your intuition, and act on it. Get second opinions or change doctors if you must.

Maintaining relations can feel like more of a high wire act than it really is. Rarely, if ever, will you need to blow the whistle loudly. Most of the time, if you aren't precipitous yet speak up when necessary, you can strike the ideal balance between maintaining cordial relations and acting in your loved one's best interest. You will be able to build a healthcare team with whom you and your loved one can feel quite comfortable.

Take a minute to reflect on your relationship to those in the medical profession. Write down whatever comes to mind without censoring your thoughts.

JOURNALING PROMPTS ON ADVOCACY

Turn to your caregiving journal and respond to the following:

1. What is your automatic stance toward doctors, nurses, and aides? Where would you place yourself on a scale between the two extremes of "blindly trusting" and "blindly critical?" Write freely about your attitudes and assumptions about those in the health care industry.

2. Who are the healthcare professionals with whom you interact on at least an annual basis? Make a list and, next to each name, write a few words to describe how you relate to them. What is your tone of voice when you speak to each? Is it meek? Authoritative? Comrade-like? What?

3. Look at the ones that you would like to consider to be on your caregiving team. How could you adjust your demeanor with each so as to enlist them even more strongly as your partners? Write down whatever thoughts come to mind.

4. When the time comes to follow an intuition, to ask clarifying questions, or to request further testing or a second opinion for your loved one, what will you need to do to maintain the assumption of partnership? What will be your biggest obstacles, both within you and without? What will it take to move forward?

Powerlessness and silence
go together."
—Margaret Atwood

FINDING & GIVING VOICE

The feeling of parenting a loved one is, for many, a wild experience of coping with mutable roles. If your loved one were to slip into a seemingly childlike moment, your first clue would probably be a change in their voice. Your voice would then change in response. At first, the trick can be to remain respectful. Though most of our elders, like us, have moments when they yearn to be pampered like a little child, they are still adults. They have lived full lives, raising families and succeeding in careers, and now at times feel weak or needy. Too many well-meaning people, including health care professionals, speak to elders as though they were children, which, for some, can be demeaning and disempowering. Practice speaking to elders respectfully.

There may also be times when your loved one will speak in a parental voice, expecting your child voice to respond, when it may be more appropriate to assert your adult boundaries. If you are spoken to as though you are a child, but you respond with your adult voice, it could feel very odd for both of you, as it did for me.

Within a couple of months, Mom's childlike glee at being cared for at the assisted living home morphed into entitlement. She referred to the aides as "the servants." When she first called me her "lifeline," my solar plexus clenched. My response was clumsy at first. One time, my "giving voice" succeeded in surprising both of us. I wrote in my diary,

> *It is midnight. It is raining. Running myself around my track of wonderings, I cannot sleep until I find an explanation. What possessed me to raise my voice to my mother? The afternoon's errands had gone much as usual. I drove, with her beside me critiquing life: 'Why on earth do they design stop lights that way? What possessed that woman to dress like that?' Back at her room, I broached the topic of summer vacation. My ideas were inspected with doubt—"Well, no, not quite right. No this one won't do"—until I heard my voice rising to fill the little room. My mother paused, astonished. Then, her voice rose behind mine, "Lower your voice!" but I was out ahead. I paused for a millisecond and loudly said, 'No, I won't!'*

That incident signaled a turning point. Rather than codependently tip-toeing around Mom, trying to make her happy, I gradually took my place as an adult by her side. Breaking the sacred childhood rule, "Don't talk back to your mother!" paved the way to speaking appropriately as an adult. As I gained strength, I saw her begin to relax. It seemed that as I became stronger, she no longer felt she had to be in control and became less anxious. Coming into my adult voice made it possible for us to be partners as we moved forward. When I didn't speak authentically, caregiving felt like a prison. When I did, it was a walk toward freedom.

In his article, *Speak Your Truth - Three Tips for Communicating Authentically,* (www. huffingtonpost.com) Mike Robbins, author and keynote speaker, distinguishes between stating opinions and speaking your truth.

"An important distinction for us to remember is the difference between our 'opinions' and our 'truth.' There's nothing wrong with having and expressing our opinions. However, many of our opinions are filled with righteous judgment and an arrogant sense that we're 'right' and those who don't agree with us are 'wrong.'

"Our 'truth' runs much deeper than any of our opinions. Truth is about how we feel and what is real for us. Truth is not about being right, it's about expressing what we think and feel in an authentic, vulnerable, and transparent way.

"This distinction is not just about semantics or words, it's a total shift in perspective and context. When we let go of being 'right' about our opinions and take responsibility for our experience, we can speak our truth from a much deeper and more authentic place. Speaking this deeper truth will not only liberate us, it has the potential to make a difference for others and bring us closer together with them."

He offers three suggestions for deepening your capacity to speak your truth with kindness, love, and authenticity

- Stop managing other people's feelings;
- Be real, not right; and,
- Practice.

One way or another, caregiving will call on you to define personal boundaries. Be clear about when you are stating an opinion, and when you are sharing a personal truth. As we speak our personal truth, we grow up. Shifting of roles and voice with your loved one can happen day to day, or hour to hour. As you move through your days together, practice activating your authentic voice when necessary. Then in the next moment, allow your loved one to be the elder and care for you. It's just one more example of the dance we caregivers do when we are at our best.

The following questions will help you to explore your role and voice.

Journaling Prompts on Giving Voice

Turn to your caregiving journal and respond to the following:

1. Does your caregiving role fluctuate between child and adult? Jot down some of your thoughts and feelings. When does your role feel appropriate? When does it not quite work?

2. What are some of the issues or topics you would like to be able to discuss with your loved one, adult to adult? Make a list.

3. Think of an instance when your voice with your loved one didn't feel right. Were you speaking authoritatively when it wasn't necessary? Or did you have a childish stance or tone when you would rather have been more adult? Write down what didn't work. Then write down what words or demeanor would have worked better for you.

4. Are there practical life considerations that your loved one is avoiding? Write about them using your adult voice, using the words you would like to say to your loved one. Try on a new voice like putting on a new pair of shoes. A live role play with a friend or counselor will free you to explore your new voice.

In this chapter we talked about how to improve your effectiveness in your life, in your relationships, and in your caregiving role.

In the next chapter, subtle and profound aspects of death and grieving will unfold, followed by guidance in when and how to step back into life.

RESOURCES

Books

The Power of Intention, by Dr. Wayne W. Dyer

Power vs. Force: The Hidden Determinants of Human Behavior, by David R. Hawkins

Seven Kinds of Smart: Identifying and Developing Your Multiple Intelligences, by Thomas Armstrong

Voice Power: Using Your Voice to Captivate, Persuade, and Command Attention,

by Renee Grant-Williams

Basic Self-Knowledge, by Harry Benjamin

The Playful Way to Knowing Yourself: A Creative Workbook to Inspire Self-Discovery, by Roberta Allen

Picking Your Battles, by Bonnie Maslin

Magazines & Websites

Listen Magazine www.listenmagazine.org

Queendom www.queendom.com

Enneagram Personality Typing www.personal-growth-counseling.com

CHAPTER SEVEN

A TIME TO DIE, A TIME TO BE BORN

When you come to the end
of all the light you know,
and it's time to step into the darkness
of the unknown, faith is knowing that
either you will be given something solid
to stand on or you will be taught to fly."
—Edward Teller

The final phase of a life varies in length from days to months, and can be a time of impromptu trouble. You may need to call on all of the skills and strengths that caregiving has taught you. When the moment of dying arrives, intervention ceases as you become a witness and supporter.

After a death, you are likely caught in the busyness of the business of it. Some of us crave solitude and silence, and so find this time a challenge. Others are grateful to have something important on which to focus. What you do now is significant because it is the final gift to your loved one. What is the appropriate service to mark the ending of a life? How do you distribute the possessions that hold a person's history? The objects may be less important than the memories, the remaining family relations more important than the things. There are many ways to re-weave a loved one's life so that it has a meaning you can carry forward.

Following all of the activity comes a phase that is yours alone. Then, finally, there is (as Hospice tells us) no emergency. You will rightly be freed to find yourself afloat in grief. We each grieve in our own way. You will find yours. At the right time, and with the wisdom that caregiving has brought, you will know your right next step and you will take it, perhaps more fully yourself than ever before.

I've told my children that when I die,
to release balloons in the sky
to celebrate that I graduated.
—Elisabeth Kubler-Ross

Coming To Death

When death is imminent, the time for heroic action has ended. Put down the work of caregiving—your job is simply to be present. To witness the journey your loved one is making on their own. To tell your loved one it is all right to go. Whoever your loved one has been for you throughout your lifetime, lovingly encourage her/him to let go. You will be helping in this final act of life.

The Hospice organization, founded to help families and loved ones cope with the end of life, has advice worth considering for how to be with a loved one who is dying:

- Touch your loved one in a way that is comforting. Let your physical presence be part of what nurtures a place of trust.
- If you can, tell your loved one you love him. If he is unable to respond, you may answer for him. "And I believe you love me too."
- If you have an experience of God's love/presence then describe it to her. If it feels natural to you, tell her that God will continue to support you after she is gone, and that she is at peace with God.
- If necessary and possible, forgive your loved one of any past estrangement/behavior/words. If he is unable to respond then you may answer for him, "And I believe you forgive me too."
- Give your loved one permission to let go. If you can, say in your own words that you trust the move from your loving hands into God's loving arms.

Mom signed her own papers consenting to a full colectomy. My sisters and husband joined me to wait out the three-hour operation. She never did regain consciousness, but hung in there, true to lines from E. Millay, her favorite poet, "With all my might, my door shall be barred. I shall put up a fight, I shall take it hard." A fierce wind blew outside, as we gathered around her bed in the Intensive Care Unit. We said, "Mom, you worked hard during your life. It's okay to go." On the third day, I returned to the hospital from church, and within five minutes she was gone. Surprised and somewhat embarrassed, I felt an exhilarating relief.

As in any major life transition, when death finally happens we are never fully prepared. For many there is a startling combination of relief and loss. When the need to struggle has ended, life can feel more spacious. You can breathe. Your loved one is no longer in discomfort. Your major work is done. Whatever your spiritual beliefs, this life cycle has come to a rightful end.

Then begins the gathering together of family members. You may participate in the design of a service to honor your loved one's life. The service frees those present, enabling them to let their loved one go. Ideally, it also confirms the remaining family connections and relationships.

Mom's service was held on a frigid morning in March. Again, wind blew with force, knocking down whole trees. The minister suggested I get the solar rainbow maker that Mom had loved and put it on the window. It seemed pointless, given the weather, yet felt right. As the minister described the wind that blew when Mom lay dying, the clouds split, letting through one shaft of light that shot down, hitting the rainbow maker. Rainbows danced around the mourners. Then a tree branch broken by a gust of wind cracked like a gunshot against the window. I said aloud, "That's my Mom!" She would have loved having that much power and the final word.

Alan D. Wolfelt, Ph.D., in his article *Dispelling the Misconceptions about Grief*, at GriefDigest.com distinguishes between grief and mourning, suggesting that grief is the container holding your thoughts, feelings and images of your experience, while mourning is the outer expression of grief. He tells us to embrace grief in small doses following our own natural process. I wrote in my diary:

> *Oh, where to start. Not knowing how to feel, I become an observer of my life. I'm in a slow motion, minimal sort of time. Not unpleasant. I'm glad that she's free, so glad that she's finally free.*

You may feel unburdened, released, even as your loved one has been released. You have graduated, have completed your good work the best that you knew how. There are a few more acts of completion. Then you will grieve in peace, and finally be free to move forward into your new life.

Reflect in your journal on endings and grief.

JOURNALING PROMPTS ON DYING

Turn to your caregiving journal and respond to the following:

1. What last words do/did you most need to say to your loved one? Many believe that an unconscious person can still hear words said to them. Others believe that, even after death, our words are heard, so it is not too late.

2. Who, in your family, might need to deal with this time differently from you? In what way? Can you make room for the differences between you?

3. If you are participating in the design of your loved one's service, which of the lessons you have learned throughout this book might ease the process? Partnering? Acceptance? Giving voice? Self-care? Others?

4. What are the emotions flowing through you? As you honor the life of your loved one, how can you also honor the job that you did during this final cycle of life?

Besides the noble act of getting things done,
there is the noble art of leaving things undone.
The wisdom of life consists in the elimination of nonessentials.
—Lin Yutang

DISSEMINATING FAMILY HISTORY

Dismantling a person's life is an important process not to be rushed. Give yourself time to sort through memorabilia, and the emotions they call up. Do the things that have stocked your loved one's life represent your history as well? Notice the ones to which you are attached. Discover the meanings that each holds for you.

If you have siblings who will join you in this process, go carefully. You could be surprised at the differences between you, even as you value the shared experience. Siblings raised in the same house can have wildly different memories and feelings. Grieving styles too can vary widely. At the same time, you can recognize in each other your shared roots.

After Mom's funeral, with its feeling of lightness and a space, weeks of spring rain hit, and my two elder sisters began their repeated visits to sort through the mountain of family things. My dissatisfaction crept in quickly. The house got messier. The lawn grew long. Flower beds filled in thickly as my dining room became clotted with ancient boxes of memorabilia. The artifacts of Mom's life passed through our dusty fingers. Silver thimbles and dim daguerreotypes of grim, faintly familiar faces. I learned that my sisters loved the history, loved reading aloud the family letters. But I wanted to look forward, not backward. The endless stories about people I had never known drove me crazy. I limited the time I spent on paperwork, instead noticing the family objects that carried meaning for me. Luckily, my sisters and I agreed easily on what each of us would keep.

Froma Walsh and Monica McGoldrick, authors of *Living Beyond Loss: Death in the Family,* address these differences in grieving styles which can leave family members feeling out of synch with each other. They suggest that, to get in synch, families must rethink and relabel their differences so that they can see them as strengths rather than weaknesses. They see dissemination of history as a process that can help with grieving. They suggest looking at old pictures, framing some to have in the home, or making an album, as well as reading old diaries or letters, sorting through memorabilia and possessions and deciding what to keep, what to pass on to others as a keepsake, and how to dispose of the rest.

These decisions are emotionally loaded. Tread lightly, with an eye to the future. This process can split the family apart as easily as bring it together. Remember, it's not about the objects themselves, but rather it is about the meanings that the keepsakes represent. If two of you are attached to the same artifact, you have choices about how you will respond. You can dicker, agreeing on compromises. You can look more closely at your feelings, perhaps finding that it is the memory that you cherish, not the object itself. Can you let such an item go? When necessary, recognize the choice between owning a thing and keeping a relationship. However this process unfolds, it poignantly encapsulates the evolution from past to future. It is a birthing.

When I couldn't stand the clutter and hours of gazing at history, I took a moment to decompress. I wrote in my journal about possessions:

> *I'll keep some poetry books of Mom's, a flower pot, a couple of tables, things that will be incorporated into my life. But is it preserving a person's essence to keep their stuff? Why try to hold on? And to what? The past drags at the heels of the future, keeps it looking back over its shoulder. It's good to let go, to be forward-looking, as Mom put it. Things are only things. Matter, as in a thing, need not matter. Matter also means to make a difference. Those who have peopled my life have already mattered—no need to commemorate them in clutter. Well, maybe one or two little special things.*

Finally the sorting was done, an auction and yard sale arranged. We then had to let go of items we had known all our lives. Sentimental value does not translate into dollar value. Who could manage to keep all those things, even if one wanted to? Better to write about them, to keep the meanings in my heart.

Hold off from returning to the routine of life. Cast a learning eye and ear to this final phase. Look for and honor the differences between you and other family members. Ask that they be respectful of your needs. Take it slowly. When approached with compassion, this ending time can serve to move the family forward in their grieving, each member alone in their personal mourning, yet together in their shared experience of loss.

Now write for a bit about what inheritance means to you, not just the inheritance of things, but also the intangible legacies.

JOURNALING PROMPTS ON DISSEMINATING HISTORY

Turn to your caregiving journal and respond to the following:

1. What have possessions meant to you throughout your life? What is the connection between your possessions and your relationships? Write about whatever comes to mind.

2. Is it your style to look backwards at what has already happened? Or do you tend to look forward, to your future? Write about how much of each would serve you best right now, and why.

3. If others are involved in the dissemination of your loved one's estate, write about their style of dealing with emotions. What do family possessions mean to them? In what aspects of the process might you respect their different ways?

4. Are there family mementos that you cling to? Write about what they mean to you. Would you want to have them at the expense of ongoing family relationships? There is no right or wrong here—only what works best for you in your life, with your future.

Nature will not let us stay in any one place too long.
She will let us stay just long enough to gather the experience
necessary to the unfolding and advancement of the soul.
—Ernest Holmes, The Science Of Mind

CLEARING THE WAY FOR GRIEF

When a loved one dies, life can feel very odd. Some people feel orphaned, or cut adrift. Whatever your history, the world is not the same without your loved one in it. Reality can blindside you when you have the urge to share something with your loved one. Emotions have a will of their own, ranging from relief to sadness to anger. It takes time to begin feeling more like yourself. The process cannot be rushed. Try to ignore grieving, and you only prolong it. Yes, this is yet another time for acceptance and awareness. The Mayo Clinic website (www.mayoclinic.org) gives us some guidelines for understanding grief and what to do with it:

"Grief is a strong, sometimes overwhelming emotion for people. They might find themselves feeling numb and removed from daily life, unable to carry on with regular duties while saddled with their sense of loss.

Grief is the natural reaction to loss. Grief is both universal and personal. Individual experiences of grief vary, and are influenced by the nature of the loss. Mourning can last for months or years. Generally, pain is tempered as time passes, as the bereaved adapts to life without a loved one."

Experts advise those grieving to realize they can't control the process and to prepare for varying stages of grief. Understanding why they're suffering can help, as can talking to others and trying to resolve issues that cause significant emotional pain, such as feeling guilty for a loved one's death.

Grieving is a moving experience in more ways than one. Feelings move through you, as you move through and beyond grief. Simple awareness of the feelings and openness to them will help them to evolve, allowing you to move forward. You can facilitate the movement.

Promoting movement during this time can be as simple as playing music, doing art, or going for walks. Suggestions on the Elizabeth Kubler-Ross website (www.ekrfoundation.org) include attending support groups, therapy, journaling, exercise, seeking solace in a faith community, and designing rituals.

A powerful catalyst of forward movement is housecleaning. It is said that clutter in your environment can block emotional progress. When we literally (or figuratively) clear the space, movement happens, both physically and emotionally. Clearing out your physical space will help you to be less disoriented and scattered, more emotionally grounded.

At that point, your thoughts are likely to turn to the rest of your life. Don't rush quickly to cram your life back into the mold of the past. You need not recreate it as it was. Some choices could be possible now that would have been untenable before.

After sorting out the family history with my sisters, the June rains gave way to sunshine. Within a couple of days, the gardens had never looked so well. It was going to be an odd year. I wrote in my diary:

Sailing in the land of grief, even this I want to do well and completely. It's clearly time to re-assess, to clear the decks. I crave isolation. Others will say of me, "She's depressed, poor thing." But that's not it. This actually is a joyous time. Mom's at peace and so am I, cleaning up, getting rid of everything that I don't love or use. I'm clearing out the dead storage of my life. If I do this well, at some point I will emerge whole and clear, and I will do something with my new life, my new self. I don't know what. Maybe writing.

We scattered Mom's ashes and dispersed her possessions. Then I declared a moratorium on commitments for the rest of the year. One year, which in many cultures is the traditional time of mourning. I wondered when it would be time to reconnect with life, but what life? Parts of my old life still cluttered my way forward. So began the second phase of decluttering—eliminating unnecessary activities.

After completing caregiving, you are not the same. So that your new life will be a reflection of who you are now, take time to become acquainted with yourself. Allow this to be an interim period, free of the busyness that would tamp down your emotions. Soon enough you will be birthing your new life. Give your internal processes their own time. Come to life slowly.

Answer the following questions to see what new space opens up for you.

JOURNALING PROMPTS ON CLEARING FOR GRIEF

Turn to your caregiving journal and respond to the following:

1. Write about the range of your emotions. How do you feel when you wake up in the morning? Or go to bed at night? For what is your soul hungry? Solitude? Children's laughter?

2. What kinds of movement would feel satisfying? Would you like to dance? Beat a drum? Sing? Go for walks? Don't worry if you feel silly or self-indulgent. This is *your* grieving time.

3. Walk through your home and notice how you feel as you enter each room. How do you feel as you look at each of your possessions? Which would you like to dispose of? Which would you like to store away? Journal freely about the process and your thoughts.

4. Make a list of the simplifications that would have the greatest impact on your inner peace.

Life has a practice of living you,
if you don't live it.
— Philip Larkin

COMING TO LIFE

After having helped in the conclusion of a loved one's life, this time is anything but ordinary. Caregiving changes a person. Though the various others in your life may be tugging at your sleeve to return to "life as usual," stop and re-assess. You are not the same. If you act without reflection, slip back into life as it was before, make choices in terms of your past, your life will end up looking much as it did. You have choices available to you now that are larger than simply making a few adjustments or reordering the pieces of your life.

These crossroads in life are an opportunity to redirect ourselves. Take time to consider who you have been, and who you will be from now forward. Looking back you can recognize your accomplishments. You might be tempted to consider what you would have done differently. The past was what it was. There is no need to clutter your heart with regrets. You may have tended to your career and/or your family. Your priorities may have included financial success, professional advancement, and/or parental competency. It was appropriate earlier in life for your focus to have been outward, on your life and the world. But doesn't life now have a different look and feel?

Be careful now not to confuse external purpose with meaning, allowing the remainder of your life to be driven by externally imposed purpose. Defined by whom? You now have different energy, wisdom, and options. Look forward with an eye for a different approach that will be in terms of who you now are.

Does your life now reflect who you are and what you believe? What would be the best use of your life and your resources? Surely you want to live fully, but who knows the secret to living life fully? Do you ruminate on life as it passes? Or do you live it more by instinct, on automatic? Whatever your style of navigation, throughout life you weave a fabric of beliefs and actions primarily intended to keep you whole and safe. But safety as an end in itself is a poor reward. Though safe, the lives of many fall short of true meaning, happiness, and fulfillment.

Where is happiness found? A prevalent myth has it that wealth is a prime source of happiness. Not so! Even Money Magazine tells us that lasting happiness is never found through acquisition. In fact, beyond a certain basic income, there is an inverse correlation between money and happiness. A popular novel, *Eat, Pray, Love*, by Elizabeth Gilbert, suggests that it is meaning that leaves us satisfied and complete.

I say that happiness is found through the generation of meanings that are attuned to our hearts, meanings to which we can then tune our lives. This requires looking inward rather than outward, seeking our inner compass that finally will orient us to our lives. Our life's work is well done when our lives are rich with meaning.

You have acquired insights and skills through caregiving that can inform your approach to designing your future. How might they serve you now?

Acceptance - Some life aspects will never be the same as before caregiving. Notice what you are resisting. Look for the opportunities for acceptance that will serve you. Some relationships have become stronger, while others may have disappeared. Hopefully, you are able to accept that you have done your best, whatever that has meant to you. To move forward, acknowledge what has been. Name the aspects over which you have had no control. It is time to let go, to accept what was, so that you can turn your vision forward.

Risk - The risks now are different from those before. These are the risks of missing out on your time of self-fulfillment. Aren't you less hampered by what others think of you? Don't you have resources available to you that you didn't have 20 years ago? Useful questions to ask yourself at this point in your life are: What have you got to lose? What do you stand to gain? What would you be willing to risk in order to have the most fulfilling time of your life? The greatest thing at risk may be never knowing your own excellence. As Marianne Williamson tells us, "It is our light, not our darkness, that most frightens us."

Change - In this time of life, change is not like that of the past. As you look back on caregiving, can you see that you have undergone a sea change? The change now available to you is not being forced on you— it is an invitation to change. You can choose to change in the direction to which you are drawn. This form of change feels like evolution. It is a blooming.

Control - During caregiving did you release some of your need to control life? The skill of allowing life to be what it is and to evolve is the key to allowing life to bloom. "Allow" is the operative word. Listen closely to your inner voice, and you will hear the way to turn. The intuition that you developed during caregiving, you now can employ on your own behalf.

Boundaries - What did you do during caregiving to clarify your personal boundaries? Did you get some practice in moderating your voice, either by speaking up or by toning down and listening? Or did you define your boundaries in some other way? The greater clarity you have gained about personal responsibility and its limits is essential to charting your new course. Acknowledging that you are not responsible for the choices others make in their lives brings you appropriately to taking responsibility for the choices you make in your own.

Generative Thinking - At this point in the mindfulness conversation, we are talking about more than inventing your experience of the present moment—we are talking about generating the rest of your life in the present moment. Observe closely the stories you tell yourself about your life and your relationships. It is too easy to decide automatically what you are required to do or think. If you do opt to take on challenges from your past, do it with a free and willing heart. What has been a burden, when freely chosen, can become a joyous endeavor. But choose carefully. You are choosing what will be true about your life now and in the future.

Not-knowing - Here is perhaps the greatest difference between life now and life before. As you allow life to lead you, relinquishing control, you find that you don't need to have all the answers. By living for a while with not knowing, you experience a new way of moving forward. Keep your eyes open and listen to your heart to learn which choices are the right ones. As you begin to follow life, the pieces fall into place. The people who will support you show up. Life becomes a joy instead of a work project. You may find yourself easily achieving things for which you struggled before. They will happen as a natural extension of your living forward, following your intuition.

The definition of "meaning" is essence, import, spirit, significance, substance and point. Meaning leaves us satisfied, complete. Imagine sitting in your rocker in the last year of your life, looking back, scanning your personal landscape of people, places and experiences. What in that picture will be most meaningful to you? What gives your life its unique substance, carries the essence of who you are? Our life's work is well done when our lives are rich with the meaningful.

Though your outward purpose may be parenting or building a marriage, helping others or following intellectual pursuits, , when you are directed by your inner compass each outward purpose is invested with personal significance. You and I are, in the end, the only possible source of meaning in our lives.

Stop here and question for a minute the parameters of your lifestyle, how they might limit you or allow for your fullest expression of who you now are.

JOURNALING PROMPTS ON COMING TO LIFE

Turn to your caregiving journal and respond to the following:

1. What aspects of your life and lifestyle are required, and by whom? Which are negotiable? Which will you re-choose? Which are you ready and willing to put behind you?

2. Do you find yourself resisting movement and change in your life? What would you like to allow into your life? What would you like to allow to move forward?

3. When you describe your life to yourself and others, what phrases do you use? What reality do these words and phrases generate? Is that a reality that you can stand behind with pleasure?

4. Since it is rare to have all the answers about what to do at this stage of life, what might be the questions that would help your life to unfold?

RESOURCES

Books

Final Gifts: Understanding the Special Awareness, Needs, and Communications of the Dying, by Maggie Callanan and Patricia Kelley

Healing After Loss: Daily Meditations for Working Through Grief, by Martha W. Hickman

The Art of Possibility: Transforming Professional and Personal Life, by Rosamund Stone Zander and Benjamin Zander

The Third Chapter: Passion, Risk, and Adventure in the 25 Years After 50, by Sara Lawrence-Lightfoot

Leap!: What Will We Do with the Rest of Our Lives? by Sara Davidson,

Magazines & Websites

Grief Digest www.griefdigest.com

Elisabeth Kubler-Ross www.ekrfoundation.org

Sarah Davidson www.saradavidson.com

The PaperRoom www.bostoncoachingco.com

Growth House (a portal for end-of-life resources) www.growthhouse.org

Midlife Bloggers www.midlifebloggers.com

Eons www.eons.com

Kids' Health - Coping with Loss and Grief www.cyh.com

Spiritual Death Midwifery www.deathmidwifery.com

AFTERWORD

Life is no brief candle to me.
It is a sort of splendid torch
Which I have got a hold of for
The moment, and I want to make it
Burn as brightly as possible before
Handing it on to future generations.
—George Bernard Shaw

By standing by Mom, I learned that her journey was her own. As Dr. Christiane Northrup said, "She had her own higher power, and I was not it." I could not change who she was, but I could ease her process. To do so, I had to stretch myself to hold her as she was, to allow room for my conflicting feelings about her. I stretched to allow her into my heart. In the end, we could connect with a look, laugh until we cried, and we were a team in the time when she needed someone most.

I am grateful. I was not being virtuous—it was just my last chance to know my mother. It was in many ways a fire walk with no guarantees, and I would choose it again. Throughout, I was determined that our time together be of some use, to balance our history with goodness.

A period of caregiving is, for many, both a time to die, and a time to be born. A time to die to what was. A time to choose to embrace what is and move forward. In the writing of this book, history is redeemed. Something fractured is made whole. Some value is reclaimed. Mom and I broke down emotional walls as I connected with myself. I am no longer the person I was, and my new life reflects the new me.

My first step was to reclaim my home. I got rid of everything that didn't matter to me, and surrounded myself with things that did. I painted the walls of my rooms in wonderful colors. We planted a memorial orchard in the bottom of our back yard, to commemorate Mom and our orchard drives.

What will your first steps be? Take the time to become acquainted with your-self. Only move ahead when you feel ready. When you do, question everything. As you move outward again into the ordinary, move mindfully. Remember that what you have just experienced, whether it was grueling or uplifting, was not ordinary and it did teach you. Acting out of who you now are, begin to craft the rest of your life in align-ment with your heart.

Now, I am not swamped by history—I can breathe. Mid-life is by nature a time of change, but by experiencing each change fully, life becomes more open, more my own. By embracing change, I peel away the meanings that have come between me and my life. I get closer to the bone of experience. I am coming to know myself and life cleanly.

For me, three years after my mother "migrated," life is a miraculous gift. I won't let anyone tinker with my joy, including myself. At 56, I am following my calling and the world is showing up in alignment with my purpose. As I share these principles of Mindful Caregiving, this book begins to have a life of its own. I am being used by it. New connections and opportunities steadily come my way. I unearth qualities and skills in myself I never knew. Underneath it all, runs the ground water of joy.

Appendix of General Support Resources

As with the individual chapter resource lists, the following collection is by no means complete. It represents a cross-section of organizations, websites, magazines, and books that can foster your further exploration.

Practical Books for Caregivers

The Complete Eldercare Planner, Second Edition: Where to Start, Which Questions to Ask, and How to Find Help, by Joy Loverde

The Alzheimer's Action Plan: What You Need to Know--and What You Can Do--about Memory Problems, from Prevention to Early Intervention and Care,
by P. Murali Doraiswamy M.D., Lisa P. Gwyther M.S.W., and Tina Adler

Eldercare 911: The Caregiver's Complete Handbook for Making Decisions,
by Susan Beerman and Judith Rappaport-Musson

The Parent Care Conversation: Six Strategies for Dealing with the Emotional and Financial Challenges of Aging Parents, by Dan Taylor

It Takes More Than Love: A Practical Guide to Taking Care of an Aging Adult,
by Anita G. Beckerman and Ruth M. Tappen

Alive and Kicking: Legal Advice for Boomers, by Kenney F. Hegland and Robert B. Fleming

Elder Rage, or Take My Father... Please!: How to Survive Caring for Aging Parents,
by Jacqueline Marcell and Rodman Shankle

Caregiver Organization Websites

National Family Caregivers Association www.nfcacares.org

Home of Children of Aging Parents www.caps4caregivers.org

AARP (Nursing Homes, Alzheimer's, Independent Living, Caregivers) www.aarp.org

Administration on Aging www.aoa.gov

Retirement Living - State Agencies on Aging www.retirementliving.com

Alzheimer's Association www.alz.org

National Association of Professional Geriatric Care Managers www.caremanager.org

The National Center for Creative Aging www.creativeaging.org

GENERAL SUPPORT WEBSITES FOR CAREGIVERS

AARP www.aarp.org

Eldercare Help www.caring.com

Family Caregiving 101 www.familycaregiving101.org

Aging Parents and Elder Care www.aging-parents-and-elder-care.com

Well Spouse www.wellspouse.org

MedlinePlus Health Information - Nat'l Library of Medicine www.medlineplus.gov

ElderSafety www.eldersafety.org

FCA: Family Caregiver Alliance www.caregiver.org

Star Life Services www.starlifeservices.com

ON-LINE COMMUNITIES FOR CAREGIVERS

The NYTimes New Old Age Blog www. newoldage.blogs.nytimes.com

Caregiving Blog www.caregivingblog.com

The Caregivers Voice www.thecaregiversvoice.com

The Family Caregiver Web www.familycaregiverweb.com

Discounted Medicines and Products www.access2wellness.com

General Support www.StrengthForCaring.com

Rosalynn Carter Institute on Caregiving www.rosalynncarter.org

National Council on Aging for benefits www.benefitscheckup.org

Strength for Caring www.strengthforcaring.com

Magazines & Articles for Caregivers

Today's Caregiver Magazine www.caregiver.com

Caregiver Today www.caringtoday.com

Coping with Caregiving www.wsradio.com

Family Caregiver Magazine www.famcaregiver.com

n4a Advocacy Action. Answers on Aging www.n4a.org

Harry R. Moody www.hrmoody.com

Videos

General Help www.caregivinghelp.org

Caregiver stress dealing with dementia www.youtube.com

Care for the caregiver www.youtube.com

Caregiver affirmations www.youtube.com

Homecare Services

Elderly Home Care www.callseniorcare.com

Eldercare Locator www.eldercare.gov

Practical Support www.lotsahelpinghands.com

Senior Home Care www.pcahonline.com

Senior Home Care – Elderly Care www.caregiverlist.com

Meals on Wheels www.nationalmealsonwheels.org

In-home Care - www.realpersonreminder.com

INDEX

A

B

C

M

N

P

Q

About the Author

Holly Whittelsey Whiteside has been a life coach for fifteen years, and was a caregiver for ten. Throughout her caregiving, she applied to herself the life coaching principles that she had been teaching others. The resulting set of thought tools now comprise the backbone of Mindful Caregiving.

The Mindful Caregiving principles are rooted in the theories of Action Language (Searles, Flores). Life coaching tools and exercises are integrated with various principles of alternative healing, mind/body practices, and New Thought.

Through private coaching, customized workshops, and her writing, Ms. Whiteside now helps caregivers to create an easier, more fulfilling caregiving experience for themselves and for their loved ones or clients. She is a certified Eden Alternative Associate.

Whiteside's writing credentials include: a collaboration with Sydney Rice-Harrild in the writing and production of *Choice Points: Navigate Your Career Using the Unique PaperRoom Process*; the on-line publication of an article series, *Mindful Caregiving: Thought Tools for Resilience*; and the reading of a personal essay on NHPR's Front Porch program. She has also been interviewed as an expert for a chapter on extreme self-care in the upcoming book, *Getting A Life*, by Nancy Christie.

Holly lives in a former one-room schoolhouse in Fremont, New Hampshire with her husband of 37 years, and two Golden Retrievers.

Ms. Whiteside's Philosophy of Work

"My work is in service of life. Wellness in caregivers breeds optimal wellness in their clients and loved ones. As caregivers learn a new language of what it means to be a caregiver, what it takes to be of greatest service, and methods for maintaining clarity of commitment, they eliminate the energy drains of caregiving. They become more available in heart and mind as they tend to their own balance and vitality."

Made in the USA
Lexington, KY
08 October 2010